FORWARD

Main Gate Tuxford Barracks

The Infantry Boys Battalion was formed in April 1952 and was in existence until 1982. There was a name change at some point and it became known as The Infantry Boys and Junior Leaders Battalion. From its humble beginnings at Tuxford Barracks in Nottinghamshire it moved three times during the thirty years it was in existence. From Tuxford to Plymouth, to Oswestry in Shropshire, where they stayed for the longest spell. They finally moved to Horncliffe before they were disbanded.

      The The Infantry Boys and Junior Leaders Battalion was the brain child of Field Marshall Sir William Slim - the Second World War hero of Burma fame. His vision was to recruit young fit boys aged fifteen to seventeen and train them to be future N.C.O.s in the Regular Army. During its existence over fifteen thousand boys from all over the British Isles were recruited and trained to a very high standard. Many of the young lads made the grade and eventually finished up as officers. The highest rank, I am aware of, is that at least

3

one made Brigadier. There were also failures as in all walks of life. The following is a true account of my eighteen months as a Boy Soldier. I wouldn't have missed it for the life of me. It was a great education and an experience that the young lads of to-day will never have.

I WAS A BOY SOLDIER

22839094 Boy Scorgie A

Bert Scorgie

Kindest Regards
Bert Scorgie

Printed and published by
For The Right Reasons
38-40 Grant St
Inverness IV3 8BN
fortherightreasons@rocketmail.com
Tel: 07717457247

I WAS A BOY SOLDIER

Speeding towards my eightieth birthday I found myself with time on my hands. This allowed me a chance to think back over the eighty years that have somehow passed so quickly. Would I have done things differently? Yes probably. I would have tweaked a few things here and there, but over all I have no complaints. I have written five books and had them published. In these books I have written about the good things but have glossed over the things that were not so good. There was to be one black cloud on the horizon, which I don't really take full responsibility for. All will be revealed as this book progresses.

Born on the fourteenth of December 1937, I made my entrance at ten past eight of that morning. My father was a regular soldier and my mother a housewife. They had been married for ten months. That was the first milestone in my life being born a healthy boy. The next milestone to be achieved was reaching the age of five. The law of the land decrees that everybody must have an Education starting off around five years of age. Due to the way the intakes worked in our area I was five years and three months old before I started school. Our lives had settled down and my mother re-married. This brought a bit of stability into the way we had been living. The previous five years had been rather traumatic for us, more so for my mother than me. She became a Widow at the age of twenty three. It's a long story already documented in an earlier book.

I enjoyed going to school but as the education got more intense, I found it very hard to grasp a lot of what they were trying to teach me. I excelled in Geography, Natural History and, in my final year, every Friday afternoon the boys had Cookery and the Girls Woodwork. I loved the cooking and still often make the meals at home. It was a great bit of skill to learn as it meant you would never be hungry provided you had the ingredients to cook a meal.

My schooling lasted for nine years and nine months. About a month before my Fifteenth Birthday I was told that I would be leaving school on the sixteenth of December. My mother had received a small pension of ten shillings (50p) per week from the Government to help with my upbringing. She was told this payment would cease on my birthday.

The Third big milestone of my life would arrive on the Fourteenth of December 1952. Nobody had ever mentioned getting employment. There were no Careers Officers in those days so here I was a month from being turfed out of school and no idea how to apply for a job, and no experience of any type of work. The only employment in our area was Farm Agricultural work. This didn't really interest me but if push came to shove this would have to be my lot.

Although I didn't feel as though I had been well educated I was a keen reader and still am. Going through a Newspaper I came upon an advert inviting youths between the ages of fifteen and seventeen the opportunity to join the Regular British Army's newly formed Infantry Boys Battalion. I filled in the coupon at the bottom of the page and posted it the same day. I must try this, all food, clothing and accommodation supplied free, you also received a weekly wage. Within days I had received an application form. It was pretty straightforward and the one question that was so easy to answer was, "Name your preferred regiment."

I had no hesitation in naming mine - The Gordon Highlanders, our family Regiment. My grandfather had been an N.C.O somewhere above the rank of Sergeant. He was wounded in the First World War and spent his final days in Erskine Ex servicemen's Hospital . My father, also a regular Gordon Highlander L/cpl, was killed in action in June 1940.

My uncle Jim, Sergeant, Gordon Highlanders, was wounded in Burma in 1943. My Uncle Sammy, Tank Corps, was killed in action in North Africa in the same year, and my uncle Dod survived the whole of World War Two. He was a Sergeant in the Royal Horse Artillery.

Our family contributed a fair amount of service and sacrifice in both World Wars, but they are all gone now and many of the questions I would like to ask will remain unanswered. My completed application form was sent by post, all I could do was sit and wait. I still had over a week before I officially left school but this momentous event would take place on the sixteenth of December, two days after my fifteenth birthday. We were requested to attend school on the sixteenth so that we could hand back any books we still had belonging to the Education Authority. In the meantime I received my instructions with a view to my becoming a Boy Soldier, I had to report to Woolmanhill Barracks Aberdeen on the eighteenth of December, I would undergo a medical examination and sit an entrance test, if I was successful I would then report to Tuxford Army Barracks in Nottinghamshire on a date to be decided, things were beginning to look up at least I had something positive to look forward to.

16th December 1952- my official date for leaving school. Our instructions were to report as usual at 9am and hand in our books and anything else belonging to the Education Authority to our teacher. On reaching the class room, the teacher told us to stack the books on our desk. After she was satisfied they were all there, we were free to go. It took me all of two minutes to get mine ready so I sat down expecting somebody to hand me a School leaving Certificate or even a reference but … nothing. The teacher had disappeared without even wishing us luck. I said my goodbyes to my class mates who were a mixture of Fisher

7

Boys and Girls, Farm Boys and Girls, one guy was joining the R.A.F boys service . That was it. We were free to go.

I had two days to wait my fate. I would either be in the Army or having to look for a job - something I didn't fancy as I had no idea where to start.

Off to bed on the seventeenth, no problems sleeping until about 5am. I woke up feeling absolutely terrible. I lay and tossed about the bed till my mother got up at the back of seven. I called her through to my room. She had one look at me and declared I had measles. She phoned the Doctor who confirmed I had a severe bout of measles and confined me to bed for forty eight hours.

Mother then phoned Woolmanhill and told them my tale of woe. She was told to keep them posted and they would arrange another date. Mid afternoon I was lying dozing off and feeling quite unwell when I heard a vehicle pull up at the door - an unusual sound in that era as there were very few vehicles about. Mother answered the knock and then proceeded to my bedroom followed by a big man dressed in Army Uniform. He introduced himself as Major so and so of the Gordon Highlanders. He claimed he was passing by and decided to give me a call. That sounded strange to me as our house was at the end of a farm track adjoining a B class road three miles off the main Aberdeen to Banff road! On top of all that there was at least a foot of snow covering the whole country side.

Personally I think he was checking up in case I had changed my mind. Who knows? My mother thought it was very good of him to show concern for my well being. Two days later I was feeling much better and managed to get about, on the 23rd December. I received a new date for my medical. It was sixth of January 1953, If successful I would catch the night train to Tuxford Army Barracks. On telling our friends and neighbors I was going to Tuxford the standard answer was "Far the bleeps at"?

When the morning of the 6th January duly arrived, I had to catch the ten thirty bus to Aberdeen so it was a long walk to the bus stop and, to make matters worse, there was at least a foot of snow. Even though there had been activity by the Council Snow ploughs it was still difficult keeping upright. I had to leave the house at nine thirty to give myself plenty time. It was a very tearful parting. My mother was distraught - no doubt she would have thoughts of my father leaving her twelve years before. He was posted to the front line of the war in France. That was the last we saw of him. He never returned. The walk to the bus was quite pleasant. It was difficult at times but it was a lovely crisp morning. I had to pass through the Beech Wood near Delgaty Castle. The scenery was like a Christmas Card. The bus was on time and I settled down for the hour or so Journey to the Granite City. I was passing through villages I had heard of but was seeing them for the first time, what an adventure this was proving to be.

Woolmanhill was a foreboding place huge in comparison to what I was used to. If my memory serves me correctly it was a Hospital but was also accommodating the Forces. The girl on reception pointed me in the right direction and I soon found the department where the recruiting was carried out. The man in charge was the same officer who had visited me when ill in bed. Once the paperwork was seen to I was medically examined, poking and pulling and peering into every opening - finally a grab and told to cough. Within a few minutes I was told that I was A1 and shown into a room where there was a desk with some papers, a pencil and rubber. I was told to start when ready and I had an hour to complete the paper, there was no brain stretching questions, all pretty straight forward, I was finished well within the hour. Again within a short space of time, I was told my examination was successful, and to proceed to the canteen and get some food. It was well after 2pm, by the time I had eaten.

I was called back to the Majors office and sworn in. I was now a member of the Regular Army signed on for eight and four. I was then given my travel Instructions: leave Aberdeen on the Eight -o- clock train, change at Doncaster get the four am train to Retford where Army transport would pick me up. I was quite nervous about the whole scenario. It was still five hours before the train left Aberdeen Railway Station - the longer I had to wait the worse the nerves got- so I decided to go for a walk. The underfoot conditions were terrible with dirty wet slush. I preferred the snow out in the country as it was all slushy and dirty in the city. Twenty minutes later I headed back into the warmth of the Barracks. The receptionist told me the Major was looking for me and to go along to his office.

I knocked and was told to enter. The Major stood up and said "Albert I have a nice surprise for you - follow me." A few doors along the corridor was yet another door. He knocked and entered. Sitting at a table were a man, woman and a lad about my age. The Major introduced me to the Barkley family and told me the son Robert would be travelling with me to-night. I nearly went into orbit what a relief that was!

Mrs Barkley asked my plans until the time of the train. I told her I would go for a meal then hang around the station. She was quite indignant when she told me I would do no such thing but would come home with them and share a meal with her family. It was getting better all the time. At about quarter past seven we left the Barkley's city centre flat and headed for the station. The adrenaline was really pumping hard as I headed into the unknown. The Platform was like the crowd going to a Football Match virtually hundreds of mostly men in Uniform from all three services.

INTO THE UNKNOWN

Bob's father advised us to get seats as at eight-o-clock it would be like a Rugby Scrum, we eventually found window seats near the front of the train. The Two Steam engines were straining at the leash as they hissed and belched out steam. There were lots of families there waving their relatives off. Every branch of the services was well represented.

Five to eight and the guard blew his whistle. Some of the couples had difficulty pulling themselves apart and of course there was the inevitable tears. I shook hands and thanked Mr.&Mrs. Barkley, then boarded the train while Bob gave his parents a hug. The doors were being slammed shut and people were still clinging to each other even through the windows as the train started to roll. The idea of the window seats was a waste of time. It was pitch dark so the only thing visible was the lights from houses or streets if passing through a village. This would be the first time in my life where I wouldn't manage to get to bed, but hopefully I would be able to snatch an hour or two as we had eight hours before we changed trains. This was my second jaunt to England. The first time I was only a few weeks old. My father was stationed in Aldershot 1938/39 but I have no recollection of that adventure.

The train clattered on reaching a fair speed. We stopped at a few stations along the way. Not many people got off but they kept packing them in. It was standing room only. The first major stop was Edinburgh where we had twenty minutes to join the scrum and grab a cup of tea - no fancy trolleys then just a kind of barrow with an urn on it and some snacks. While we were stopped a rather surely fellow about our age grabbed a seat in our carriage. He didn't acknowledge us so we left him to his own devices. He was soon asleep.

11

Onward we sped and reached Newcastle at some ungodly hour of the night, again there was a barrow selling tea so I jumped off the train and managed to grab two cups before it was time to move on, the person manning the Barrow was an elderly man. It was freezing cold and, he had an enormous drip to his nose as I sipped my tea I wondered how many drips had landed in people's tea!

We had to leave that train at Doncaster and catch what was known as the Milk Express. It seemingly delivered milk churns at the various stations along the way. It was nearing six am when we eventually arrived at Retford Station.

I was beginning to feel the effects of the lack of sleep and was quite delighted to note that our transport in the form of a fifteen hundred weight truck was waiting for us. The driver had the engine running so it was lovely and warm. We clambered aboard and took off. The roads were none too clever and the driver had to use all his skills to keep us on the road, it was quite slippery. We were chattering away to the driver telling him about the journey from Aberdeen when he suddenly turned to face us. His comment was " Are you sure you're not effing Swedes! I don't understand one effing word you are saying!"

I didn't bother to explain that we were from the North East of Scotland where we have our own lingo it was easier just to shut up and say no more.

Eventually we arrived at the village of Tuxford. It was a sizable place straddling the A1 road. Half way through the village we turned to our right. Negotiating the bend was rather tricky on the icy snow covered road, but we made it, and proceeded to drive at a crawl about two hundred yards along that road. In front of us we spied the lights of Tuxford Barracks, the first thing that entered my head was their likeness to a German POW Camp - Stalag Tuxford my new home for the foreseeable future! We soon arrived at the

12

Guardroom, where we were booked in by a Regimental Policeman. The Guardroom had one or two inmates who were peering at us through the barred windows. From there we were driven to the Dining room. It was breakfast time and the place was heaving with lads tucking into their food. We were told to get in line and help ourselves to whatever took our fancy.

I was gobsmacked at the array of food. At home it was either porridge or the Scottish Cuisine Brose. In front of me was Cereal,,Porridge ,Sausage, Bacon, Egg, Beans, Tomato and Fried Bread - wow!

We sat at an empty table sticking out like a sore thumb but we were soon put at ease when one of the established lads came over to talk to us. He was Dave Taylor, a huge Londoner.

He must have been a lot older than us as he sported a fairly well grown mustache. He introduced himself and told us he was Badged for the Gordon Highlanders like we were. He shook hands and welcomed us to Tuxford.

Within half an hour the dining room was nearly empty with only Bob and me left. We were told to wait and our platoon Sergeant would come for us. He duly arrived and took us to our new accommodation. It was totally empty except for a stack of empty bed frames and a locker to go with each bed. Our Sergeant told us to start setting up the beds, firstly showing us what to do. The rest of the lads would be arriving during the day.

Around 11 am the door of the Billet opened and lo and behold the guy who entered was familiar, it was none other than the kid who had boarded the train in Edinburgh. He was Tommy Davidson, he never acknowledged us when he boarded the train and he slept most of the way. He was still sleeping when we left the train at Doncaster. He had slept all the way to Peterborough. He turned out to be a grand fellow, fitness fanatic who went on to win an ABA Boxing Title along with another lad called Taffy Ryan.

By lunch time we had a complement of over twenty guys. There were a few stragglers to come - two from Ireland and one from Jersey. At lunch time we were told to make our way to the Dining Room. After eating we were told to gather back in the billet from there we would proceed to the stores where we would be kitted out.

At one thirty a rather untidy squad of Boys attempted to march in step to the Quartermaster's Store. They started to throw kit at us which we stuffed into the Kit Bag. The sizes were guessed by appearance and we would only know if they fitted when we tried everything on. Loaded down and looking like a Second Hand Clothes market stall, we headed back to the billet where we were given a demo on how to fold our kit and bedding. It was now down to us and we were expected to be ready to go on Parade at eight am next morning.

Everything was spread out on the bed so it had to be cleared by lights out at ten-o -clock, folded and stacked in the locker as we were instructed. The bed pack was another kettle of fish. It was rather tricky to get it folded as the regulations required.

The dress uniform was a left over from The Somme by the look of it and the feel of the cloth! Rough as a badger's arse was the description I overheard. Then the shirts: thick Khaki flannel so rough you could have sandpapered a piece of wood with them. Then the boots: one black pair, one brown pair. Both had to be bulled and left smooth and highly polished, this would eventually be achieved after many hours and many tins of Cherry Blossom shoe polish. Our wages 17/6 (75p), 10/-(50p) was paid directly to us and the remaining 7/6 (35p) was paid into a Post office Savings account (POSB) . The first week we had a huge pay out as we had to purchase Blanco White and Khaki, Boot Polish,

Brasso and the cloths to apply the stuff. So not much left of the first 10/- pay packet. We were given our savings in the POSB when going on leave. Sorting out the kit was hard work, and just for a bit of variety we were told we had to attend muster parade at 8 am next morning wearing our Denims. They were the most ill fitting of our kit along with the thick flannel shirts, they seemed to have been tailored to fit a six foot guy.

My vital statistics according to my pay Book were height five foot three, weight eight stone one pound and waist thirty one inches. So the shirts reached my knees otherwise the rest were as near as dammit.

It had been a hectic day and with us travelling overnight. By nine -o-clock I was shattered and was looking forward to lights out. My kit was folded and stacked away, just the boots to bull, the blancoing to be done and try and borrow an Iron as the best dress was very creased. Oh and the beret to shrink as it resembled a flying saucer.

YOU'RE IN THE ARMY NOW

Breakfast over the billet was a hive of activity as lads rushed about getting ready for our very first Muster parade. We were then going on the Drill Square for a session of square bashing just a taste of what was in front of us.

I'm sure we were a comical lot as we tried to keep in step. The co-ordination was missing in many of the guys but practice would improve our standards. The guys who had been Army Cadets were head and shoulders above the rest of us but it would all slot into place eventually. Our first Muster parade over now for the Drill Square for a spell of Square Bashing . About twenty minutes of being shouted at and in some cases humiliated we started to get a feel for doing things correctly. The square was pretty slushy as there was still some snow on the ground. This didn't help with halting when ordered but we survived and were marched back to our billet where we were to have a barrack room inspection, this was to find out if we had stacked everything correctly. You would have thought there had been a hurricane breezed through our Billet where the Bed pack didn't come up to standard. It was chucked on the floor as was some of the locker contents - very few bed spaces were left untouched .We had an hour to put the damage right. T

Thankfully we all passed second time around but we were warned of the consequences if we got it wrong again. The rest of the day was spent working on our kit, our first official parade was on Sunday when we had to attend Church that would be interesting.

The Boys Service was run along the same lines as school. our days were divided into periods, Square Dashing, Physical Training, Education, Field Craft (map reading etc), Route Marches, Sport and various other activities. In the evenings there were various night classes if you were that way inclined ie Basket Weaving, Scottish Country Dancing to name a couple.

As I mentioned before to make life a little more difficult we were given two pairs of Boots: one brown and one black. The brown ones were supposedly Surplus Officers Issue. We had to make them black!

As they were the smartest, we used them as Dress to go with our Uniform. It needed about fifty tins of cherry Blossom to get them black all over and the hours of our time was phenomenal but with no Television and the Radio was piped so you had to listen to what somebody else had chosen. Bulling the Boots passed the time.

Saturday was the day off but we still had to be out of bed at reveille six am and then a maniac Corporal screaming like a Banshee made sure you were on the floor by Six -O-Two. My memory is a bit hazy but I don't think we had a long lie. It was the same time every day of the week. But, whatever else, we had plenty of Polishing, Bulling and keeping the Billet tidy to fill our day adequately.

I was finding it hard going. After all I was just past my Fifteenth Birthday so in reality still a kid.We had never had to do any of the things we were now being asked to do. It would be a struggle to get everything ready before Church Parade on Sunday. One of the lads had an older brother - also a Boy Soldier - we were able to borrow an iron from him so yet another chore was added to our repertoire, it took me a while to master the art of ironing.

Before we knew it, Sunday morning had arrived. It was quite exciting our very first Parade. We had to be ready for around ten am so in theory we had bags of time. But time is so deceiving and creeps away from you if you have a target to meet. Our Platoon Sergeant was soon shouting at us to get on parade, he had a quick swatch at us to see we were properly dressed, then marched us to the Drill Square, where the rest of the battalion was milling about as they formed up in Numerical order.

We were No. Fourteen Platoon C Company. A company had moved to Harrogate the previous year as Tuxford filled up with new intakes. The RSM Tony Martin called us to attention and we were off. It was quite a feeling, we were at the tail end and were just getting the feel of this marching lark. It was about one and a half miles to the Kirk still in mid winter so it was quite cold but you never felt it while marching. About twenty minutes later we were fell out and in an orderly manner entered the old church. It was packed. Just over an hour later we were on our way back, just in time for Lunch.Our first parade had gone fine without any major disasters, back in the Billet it was down to the Kit cleaning and polishing again.

Monday Morning would bring a whole new dimension to my life. I had never tackled anything like this before. The first shock was the having to rise at six am, then the big rush to get dressed before heading to the Dining Hall for breakfast. Although it was nearly two hours before we were on muster parade we needed all our time.

With a little experience we could overcome the difficulties we had encountered over the first few days. We had now been allocated numbers, it was given to me sixty five years ago but it comes to me in a flash 22839094. It's strange how that number sticks in your head compared to a password which is gone in minutes - for me anyhow.

Our day was taken up with Square Bashing, then Two hours of Education. In the afternoon we had a Hockey Match - the first time for me but I really enjoyed it. By the time we showered and changed the working day was over, couldn't wait to get into Bulling the boots again.

18

I had been in Tuxford four days and it had been full of shocks, surprises and all sorts of new things I didn't know existed. Even some of the new words we learned were alien to some of us. The biggest shock to-date happened on my second day as a Boy Soldier remembering I was only fifteen years and twenty seven days old.

My next adventure kind of gobsmacked me. We were ordered to line up outside the Billet at two pm, no clue given as to why. We came to attention. right wheel and we were off down through the barracks towards the Storage Area. We arrived at a rather small building, above the door it said Armoury. My ignorance kicked in right away, I had no idea what an Armoury was. Anyway it was quite shocking to see rows and rows of point three o three rifles. We were about to be allocated one each. Nobody had mentioned that we would one day probably have to shoot people.

A shiver ran down my spine when I was handed one and told to move to the next counter where I was handed an evil looking Bayonet, on to the next counter and we were handed a shoulder strap and scabbard. We shuffled along to the last counter where all the numbers were logged and we had to sign for the goods. Back at the Billet, we had been away about an hour. We were told to stow our rifles in the rack provided for them. Then it was lecture time and a demonstration on how to clean and oil our lethal weapon.

The only gun I had ever fired was at the fairground side shows, knocking over cans with an Air-rifle. After severe threats as to our fate if the Rifle was not kept up to scratch, we were dismissed and given the rest of the day to give the rifle its first clean and remove any grease.

The sergeants words as he left was " Your rifle is more important in your life than your mother ever was so make sure it is lovingly looked after. It will be inspected weekly, heaven help any body with a dirty rifle". I think we all get the message. Sergeant didn't like dirty guns. Our full complement of bodies numbered twenty five: six Scots , two Irish. The rest were from England and Wales. Within a week we were reduced to twenty four when one of the Scots lads disappeared discretely.

We returned to the billet for a change of gear mid morning on our second official day and were surprised to see an empty bed space, what's going on here? was the comment passed as we looked on only the empty bed frame and an empty locker. It would be later on in the day we would find out the answer to the mystery.

The missing lad was a fellow Scot, quite a small guy, very quiet. I didn't get to know him, Poor fellow was a bed wetter and, after about three days his bedding was saturated. I felt heart sorry for that poor kid. There is nothing worse or more humiliating than bladder and bowel problems. In modern times with the technology available I'm sure they could have done something to help this lad but the way things were back then you just had to accept it. The Army were very understanding and got the Laddie away from where he may have been humiliated by his fellow Boy Soldiers. Some of them were capable of being nasty. All his Army gear and bedding was incinerated, the bed space was soon filled by a Lad who had transferred from the Royal Artillery Boys Service.

Our third day I felt reluctant to get up. The bulling of the boots was beginning to grind on me and it was quite a long day from six am till ten pm, very tiring for a young fellow like me. So I was dragging my heels that morning and starting to run out of time. It was getting near to ten to eight, our time for going on Parade. I was still tidying up as we started to head for the door. Formed up in three ranks outside the Billet waiting for the Sergeant and his Corporal to appear.

Next moment the peace was shattered as the Sergeant, screaming like a banshee, came marching along the ranks. He stopped at me and continued his tirade of abuse. I could feel the spit splashing on my face but he was in such a wrath I had difficulty getting the gist of what was wrong. In my rush to be on time instead of folding my pajamas and stacking them in the locker I had pushed them under the bed pack, wow our Sergeant was upset and accused me of taking the piss. For my misdemeanours I was on a charge and had to appear in front of our Company Commander at eleven am.

I was completely mesmerized and had no idea what all this jargon meant, the Platoon Corporal explained it all to me and assured me I would most likely be put on Jankers, another new word. This should be interesting.

My whole morning was in turmoil as I worried myself near to death, wondering what fate would befall me. Listening to my Platoon mates the punishment was wide and varied from six lashes with the cane (still legal in nineteen fifty three) to a week in the cooler.

My best mate said I would be admonished as it was my first offence ie a slap on the wrist. Their suggestions did not make my feelings any better. I must have looked at my watch a thousand times as I waited for twenty to eleven to arrive. Then all of a sudden it was here, I excused myself and hurried along to the Company Commander's office. He was a Major Smythe of the Seaforth Highlanders. We were both Jocks so he might take pity on me,(tongue in cheek) . There were four or five of us. Our Company Sergeant Major Bunny Warren was there he gave us the once over to make sure we were properly dressed.

At eleven he called us to attention, then with much stamping of feet the first defaulter and his escort were marched in, four minutes later he was wheeled out and the next one was called in. I glanced at my watch. We had been there sixteen minutes and it was my turn next. I was called to attention and my escort lined up, one in front one behind and we were quick marched into the C. Cs office all together there were six of us, C.C , Platoon Sergeant, a clerk, me and two escorts.

The Platoon Sergeant gave his spiel, about what a naughty Boy I had been and, in spite of being shown on umpteen occasions how to fold and stow my kit, this morning I had stuffed my Pajamas under the bed pack, totally against company rules. The Major pondered what he had been told, scribbled something on a pad then looked at me, he asked if I had anything to say for myself, to which I answered no Sir.

He looked up and announced three days confined to Barracks. I was marched back to the corridor and dismissed. The platoon Corporal explained what C. B was all about. "You report to the Guard Room starting at six fifteen am then again at six pm in the evening, you will be allocated one and a half hours of Fatigues by one of the R.Ps. It's in your own interest to be on time otherwise you could end up on further charges. After your Fatigues are completed you return to the Guard Room where you will be dismissed.Then you report back every half hour until nine thirty pm, do you understand that ? You will carry on for the next three days. Keep your wits about you lad and your nose clean and you will be ok."

I was a bit down after two days experience and had the added ordeal of having to report to the Guardroom at six pm where I would learn my fate. Facing the unknown is never easy. It was on my mind the rest of the day. Five pm arrived. Time to go for my tea at quarter to six. I made tracks to the Guard room. It was a three minute walk. So I arrived early. A little jumped up Lance Jack in the Norfolk Regiment was the Regimental Policeman on duty. He told me in the most ignorant of tones to line up and wait for the rest to appear, eventually there were about six or eight of us.

This little prick of a man had us coming to attention and standing at ease for about five minutes before allocating us our work station for our Jankers. I was quite pleased with my assignment. I was to report to the cook house to a Corporal Harris (later Sargent). He was a typical Chef, a short round jovial guy. At least he was civil. He asked me my name and commented, "Young Jock, can you peel spuds?" "yes Corporal I did many times for my mother" "right lad follow me".
He showed me into a small room where there was a strange looking machine in the corner and a zinc bath full of potatoes just below it. The Corporal explained the machine peels the spuds but cant remove the eyes and rotten bits, that was my job. I soon got the hang of it.There was only one and a quarter hundred weight soit shouldn't take long. Exactly one hour later I was complete. I had a smoke then went and found Corporal Harris. He could hardly believe what I was telling him as it usually took other guys a couple of hours to perform the task. He told me to go and have a seat in the Dining Room and he would be with me in a minute or two. I still had twenty minutes to go before my time was up.Suddenly Corporal Harris appeared with a mug of tea and the biggest bacon and egg sandwich I had ever seen. Wow! He just said " Here get that down you." What a saint!

Back at the Guard Room our tormentor was waiting for us. As was usual he had some sarcastic comment to make. He must have felt good slagging off mere school boys. He had us doing a couple of drill movements before dismissing us. We had to report back in one hour. In the meantime I could get on with my chores, getting my kit up to scratch. The rest of the evening passed without incident and I paid two more visits to the Guard Room before lights out. My next visit was at Six Fifteen. Next morning I would try and get up early to give myself plenty of time - mustn't give them any more opportunities to put me on more charges. The smiling assassin was waiting for us, it was bitterly cold so he didn't keep us hanging about, roll call and dismiss. I could then get on with the rest of my day.

The day soon passed and it was coming up to six pm. We were lined up in front of the Guard Room waiting to be allocated the evenings fatigues. I was all primed up to head for the Kitchen and another session spud bashing, but no. When my name was called along with two others we were told to head for the Admin Block - disappointing no Bacon Sarny to-night. The Admin Block consisted of a row of Offices , Commanding Officer, Adjutant, Pay Office, Admin and the Guard Room.

Our task was to dust, polish and tidy the various offices. My two companions, who I had never set eyes on before, had a bit of dispute as to who would do the C.Os office. I had no preference. All I wanted was to get my hour and a half over and get back to working on my kit. I eventually found out the attraction of the C.Os Office.

Our Commanding Officer was Major Nixon of The R.U.R. He had been wounded in Korea. His big vice was that he chain smoked forty to sixty cigarettes per day. When it came to cleaning out his office, his ash tray would be over flowing with dog ends. Seemingly the guys used to keep the dog ends and roll fags out of them. They were welcome to them. My twenty Park Drive now and again satisfied me.

As I headed back to the Billet I had a spring in my step. One more day and freedom again. My final day was Saturday, our tormentor in the Guard Room gave me the job of cleaning the MI room for my final task. It wasn't too bad but I was happy to see the back end of it. Iit was a short sharp lesson for me as it used up a lot of my precious time. Next morning was Sunday and we had Church Parade. At least we would get out of the gates for a couple of hours. We could have a good view of the country side as we marched back, a change from looking at the walls of the Billets.

The rest of the Month passed without incident until the night of the thirty First January. A bit of a storm was brewing. The wind was quite strong, causing great difficulty keeping upright.By the morning it was a real hurricane and very difficult to move about. This lasted most of the day of the first of February but had disappeared over night.

Although the wind had been ferocious, no visible damage had occurred. The storm had passed and the weather was peaceful again.

Two or three days later I was in the recreation room looking at the books in the library when I noticed a news paper. Glancing at the headlines I near passed out. It was giving all the details of the chaos caused by the storm. There were hardly any trees left standing in the North East of Scotland where my folks lived, but worse was to follow. Although we had no damage or injuries to anyone it appears the rest of the country had suffered damage and tragedies.

The Ferry from Ireland had sunk and one hundred and thirty three people had lost their lives. Nineteen deaths recorded in Scotland,,three hundred and seven in England. Worst hit were the Low Countries: Belgium and Holland. They had suffered severe flooding, and also recorded over two thousand two hundred and twenty five deaths. It was absolutely devastating. there were also people killed in Lincolnshire and Norfolk which were pretty close to where we were based.

After reading the newspaper, my main concern was how did my folks fare at home? The most frustrating part was there was no way to contact home other than write a letter No mobile phones, television or even a personal radio and there was no public phone boxes in the Camp - not that it would have been any great help as my parents didn't have a phone.

The nearest was the Farmer's private phone and they would not ask to use it unless it was a life or death situation. I had just to content myself with writing to my mother to find out the latest news. It was ten days before I had word on the havoc caused by the January Gales, and was delighted to hear that, although we had lots of damage and whole wooded areas flattened, there were no casualties.

I had settled into life as a Boy Soldier with no real problems except that I could get slightly home sick now and again. I attended the night classes with my Glaswegian Mate Phillip. We were next bed to each other. We did Scottish Country Dancing and Basket Weaving . We were now on top of our kit with only the Boots proving a handful. Cherry Blossom cost us a fortune, we had a grand Squad of lads no bullying, no thieving, everybody pulling together. Our next big event on the horizon was our first leave.Our ten weeks basic training would be over mid March. We were then due ten days leave.

The training was quite enjoyable especially the Education. Our Tutors were Sergeants in the Education Corps. They seemed to have a better system of teaching than our school teachers had. I looked forward to my Educational Sessions. I was studying for my Third Class Army Certificate, I would be sitting the exam in June. Our first leave was due on the second Friday in March just about ten days away. The excitement was beginning to mount and I was looking forward to seeing my family again but first I would have to endure a twelve hour journey.

ESCAPE

We were to be set free at ten am on the Friday so the Barracks were in Chaos as the lads prepared to head off in different directions. I was probably one of the farthest from home but we had two Irish lads in our Platoon so they may have had a long haul to get home also. A few of the more brainless ones bought bottles of Pale Ale and were staggering about the Station as though they were drunk. We had to endure their company as far as Newcastle. The Army had supplied trucks to take us to the station at Retford. There were quite a few guys heading north so we managed to fill a few carriages. Our first change was at York. We had a couple of hours there so we had a wander round the Town before we caught a connection to Edinburgh, where we had to change again, this time to Dundee where we finally caught a train to Aberdeen.

Time was dragging on and I realised I would never be able to catch a bus home to Turriff. In fact it was near two am when we finally landed in Aberdeen. One of the lads who stayed in the City gave me an idea. He told me to go to the Post Office Sorting Office and see if I could cadge a lift in the mail van.

My luck was in for a change. The man loading the van was going to Banff. I gingerly asked if there was any chance of a lift as far as Turriff. He reluctantly agreed, pointing out it was against the rules but if I walked to the end of the street he would pick me up in ten minutes. What a relief! Otherwise I would have to hang about until at least six am, it was only the back of three then. The journey to Turriff was quite hairy to say the least, the road was fairly slippery but we made it without incident. The Postman dropped me off at the end of the road I needed to take to get home. It was a four mile hike but at least the snow had gone. Quarter to five in the morning found me marching up the B class road to the farm where my parents lived. As I walked on my own with not another soul to be seen, I noticed something strange had happened since I had left home. The road used to be an avenue of the most wonderful beech trees, many years old. I used to love walking along that road in the summer - nature at its very best.

But, wait a minute something is wrong. I could see the sky in the early morning light. This was something that never used to happen. It suddenly dawned on me that the lovely Beech trees were gone, lying flat on their side. This was the aftermath of the January Gales. In daylight it looked like a bomb site. The wind is a powerful medium.

I arrived home just on six am. My parents were just getting out of bed. It was a pretty emotional reunion. My mother soon had the frying pan going as she cooked me some breakfast. Soon the rest of the siblings were crowding round me. I had brought them all a small present so they were delighted to see me.

My ten days soon passed and it would be time to return to Tuxford - an ordeal in itself. To avoid wasting a day of my leave I would travel back on the Monday. We had to book in by ten pm. In order to achieve this I had to be in Aberdeen to catch the six am train. This meant that I would have an overnight stay. Nobody could afford bed & breakfast then so the only alternative was to kip down in the Station Waiting Room. Unfortunately another fifty or so people had the same idea. When I arrived about eleven pm there wasn't one inch of vacant space, people lying everywhere. I had no alternative but to find an empty bench and make the best of it. Anyone who has experienced Aberdeen Station at mid-night in the middle of March will tell you there were no comforts, the freezing cold was murder. All you could do was walk around and try and keep warm, I did have a seat in the Toilets for a while. The stench was easier to put up with than the cold.

Around two thirty am a train arrived. I had a walked along the platform just out of nosiness but not many passengers got off. It was a mail train. I stopped and had a look inside the carriages. Suddenly I sensed somebody behind me. This voice said " Hive yea got a licht min?" - standing in front of me was a short, rather scruffy looking guy with an unlit cigarette in his mouth.

Without answering I fumbled in my pocket and produced a box of matches.Tthe guy handed me a cigarette and said "Here min hiv a fag". He then proceeded to ask me my business why I was there and when did I get a train. He seemed quite a friendly chap but he was reeking of booze. After about ten minutes conversation he said he was waiting on relatives but they hadn't arrived on the last train so he would just hang aboot till the 5 am got in. He then made a play about feelin the cauld and suggested we go for a walk round the Station explaining that you could go right round. It would take about half -an-hour.

My friend kept staggering into me. He seemed quite drunk. Along the back of the Station there was a grassy bank. He suggested we should have a seat and another fag. I had no sooner sat down when I felt his hand go between my legs and he said "Tell me aboot aw the Quines (girls) you were oot wie when yea were hame."

I got such a shock I near passed out. I jumped down off the bank and ran like the devil until I got back to the Station. Reflecting on what happened when I got my breath back I couldn't believe I had been so bloody naive, but we weren't used to people like that little weed. We knew everybody at home and trusted them completely.

On telling the lads back in camp one lad remarked, "He would have been a bloody arse bandit, I hope you left him with sore knackers." Well I didn't try to do anything other than run he was an adult man and would probably have got the better of me for strength. Often you read in the Press about some innocent boy or girl who met a complete stranger and finished up murdered. You think how could they have been so stupid as to go with that low life? Having experienced it I would say it is very easy to get drawn in. loneliness is a good starter. I was lonely the night I was picked up and maybe I was lucky my friend was drunk which slowed down his movements.

I boarded the six am train for Doncaster. It was about an eight hour journey. I had company as at least a couple of guys boarded the train before we left Aberdeen.. The journey to Tuxford was uneventful and we arrived at around six pm - plenty time to get our Kit ready for the first day back.

We were soon back in the swing of things. Our training was quite intensive both Military and Educational but I was enjoying it the company of the other lads. They were excellent - no arguments or dissent . Education was a big thing and we were to sit our third class exams near the end of June. Before that we had a Coronation to witness as the Young Queen Elizabeth would be crowned. This was to take place on the second of June 1953, if I remember correctly.

We had some of the older boys lining the route. We were granted five days extra leave. I decided to go and stay in Perthshire with my aunt and uncle. It was a much shorter distance to travel in view of us only having five days leave.

The locals held a sort of fete. It was quite an enjoyable afternoon with all sorts of competitions for the kids. There was Fancy Dress, Games and a huge spread of food. Then in the evening they had a dance in the local hall - a very enjoyable week-end.

There were many funny incidents in the Barracks but we also had our share of sadness. Such an event happened one evening when one of our number took his own life. I briefly knew Syd. He had spent a couple of nights in our Billet as we had a spare bed. I just remember the lad. He would be sixteen/seventeen maybe. Obviously he must have had problems when he went to such drastic lengths as ending his life.

It was obviously well planned as it happened during a Fire Drill when there was a bit of turmoil and noise. He was found the next morning with his rifle beside his body. It always grieves me when I hear of people ending their own lives. I had many friends and relatives who didn't get the chance to end their lives. It was done for them. They would have wanted to stay a while longer - sad times.

We spent the next week after the death practising for a Military Funeral, up and down the Drill Square carrying a make shift coffin. The bit that sticks in my memory was the stifling heat.With our thick khaki uniform it was pure murder. Syd was buried privately in his home town of Hull with no fuss.

One of the funny incidents, and there were many, happened on our first exercise. This was when we hid behind trees and attacked the Enemy who were still Germans. It was quite good fun and a chance to dirty our rifles so that we could clean and oil them when we got back to the billet. We had a small area of scrub where we did our battle training. All was going well until there was a wail from behind a bush and a lad, Brian, appeared with his rifle in two halves, barrel in one hand, butt in the other and he was crying his eyes out, terrified at the consequences he could expect for breaking his best friend.

This lad was not the brightest and the Sargent Major referred to him as Pea Brain. I never did find out how he managed to break the rifle but it was maybe lucky he wasn't firing it at the time. No recriminations were taken against

31

poor Brian.

We had a full program ahead of us for the remainder of the summer. It would take up quite a lot of our time. Firstly we had a visit and inspection from the Chief Of The Imperial General Staff (CIGS) none other than Field Marshal Sir William Slim, as we mentioned before, a war hero in the Burma Campaign in World War Two. He was the founder of the Infantry Boys Battalion. is arrival by Helicopter caused a bit of a stir as many of us had never seen one before. It was parked on the football field with a sentry watching over it.

Field Marshall Sir William Slim of Burma visit to Tuxford 1953

We never got within two hundred yards of it. Compared to modern day choppers it was pretty pre historic. We had spent a week spitting, polishing and painting. The camp had to sparkle for that occasion.

There was a bit of excitement when a premises in the

village was burgled. The Lads in the camp were checked out but I don't really remember the outcome. Something tells me it was a Glaswegian Lad who we will hear about later on.

Next on the agenda was the Third Class Education Examination. It was all nerves and Adrenalin as we got that ordeal behind us. I so wanted to pass in view of my dismal School record. I was finding the Education much easier than I ever found at School.

In between times I was offered a place on a sailing boat on the River Trent one Saturday. I had never tried sailing before so it would be a new experience. Sadly sailing was not for me. I found it quite boring. You needed the enthusiasm and dedication. I had neither and was never asked back again. I got word that my Exam had been successful and I had passed all eight subjects.

Somewhere along the line we had a change of Commanding Officer. Major Nixon disappeared and his place was taken by Lt Colonel Kinderslay Highland Light Infantry. The next big event on the Calendar was the first Passing Out Parade. This was for lads who had reached their

Passing Out parade Tuxford circa 1953

Seventeenth Birthday and were ready to move on to their chosen Regiment. There were many days of practice. Our

33

Platoon was not involved in the actual parade but we were posted around the Square. There were still three weeks to go before the Parade so the Lads had time to practice. At the end of the week after the P.P. We were off for two weeks leave. The day of the big parade finally arrived. The Drill Square was set out with seating along the side where the Dias was situated. Quite a lot of relatives, girlfriend's etc were there. The Military band of the Sherwood Foresters were to provide the music during the ceremony. The sun was shining. Everything looked perfect for the first passing out Parade.

The salute was being taken by Field Marshal Harding assisted by our new C.O. There was lots of hustle and bustle on the drill square as spectators milled about trying to get the best seats. The band of the Sherwood Foresters were in position just off the Drill Square, waiting for the nod to strike up. The magic hour arrived and the band struck up the first score of music. The battalion entered the square from behind the dining area. They were off into the well rehearsed routine. The whole parade lasted about an hour. They were ready to be dismissed, but the final order of the day was not as it should have been. Well you needed one hiccup! Otherwise it would have been near perfect.

Charlie Moss the Boy R.S.M. called the Battalion to attention, right turn and dismiss, but Charlie boobed at that point. He should have got them to shoulder arms before the right turn but he forgot. Pity after a near perfect parade.

Any how nobody panicked and they marched off with their rifles at the long Trail (I think that's the term for that movement.) Parade over, we were free to wander about showing any visitors round the camp and of course there was lunch to be taken.

In the evening we were in for a surprise. There was a dance in the Gymnasium so we all headed there. The Foresters were again providing the music. Suddenly there were about four or five coach loads of Lassies about our ages. They were from local villages round about. At least we didn't have to dance with each other thank goodness. I had a lovely evening in the company of a young lassie from Retford. made a date to meet her after I came back off leave. We met up two or three times on a Saturday but had to part company due to finances. I couldn't afford the bus fare. It was about two and a half pence each way. Yes folks that how rich we were.

Into the new week the Passing Out parade was now history. Our main outlook was getting to Friday and off home for a spot of leave, but things are never straight forward and we had another piece of Drama in our ranks before we would leave for home.

Phillip, who occupied the next bed space to me, came charging through the door of the billet on the Wednesday after he had knocked off, swearing and kicking things about.

I had never seen him so upset. Phil was usually the joker in the pack, full of fun, a real smashing guy, always laughing and if there was devilment he would be in the thick of it. What could be wrong ?

Once he calmed down he explained his predicament. He had fallen foul of the establishment and found himself up on a charge.I can't remember what it was but anyhow he was up in front of the Company Commander in the morning. He was sure he would get confined to Barracks. The verdict was always guilty. Nobody ever got admonished. The reason being they needed bodies to do the cleaning and polishing so what better way but to find the defaulters guilty.

Phil was wished luck by most of the lads as he headed for the C. Cs office. Twenty minutes later he was back, Confined to Barracks for seven days, or he was given an alternative, six strokes of the cane (yes folks Corporal punishment was still administered in certain cases). Phil opted for the cane and at nine-o-clock on the Friday

35

morning he had to report to the Gymnasium to receive his punishment. There were another two guys on the same mission. At least one of them travelled from Harrogate from where A Company was stationed. Trust Phil he was a lovely guy full of beans but very naive easily led, this would lead to his downfall..

Anyhow we were all waiting to see how Phil got on. We were all packed ready for the off at mid-day. Phil appeared back at ten-o-clock. He was rubbing his rear-end. The guys were firing questions about the procedure etc. One guy suggested Phil should drop his trousers so that we could see the damage done to his arse. He was reluctant but eventually he gave in and and showed us the weals across both buttocks. It was rather barbaric and that was the only incident of the cane being used as far as I am aware. Your parents had to sign a form consenting to this punishment being used and also to allow you to smoke, my dear old mother did not consent to me being caned. Bless her.

As usual the leave passed way too quickly and, before you knew it, was time to head back. No incident to report about the journey on the way home. We had to stand most of the way as the train was full of drunken sailors. Their ship had docked in Portsmouth and they were going home for a spot of leave they were rowdy and most untidy by the time we got to Aberdeen the train was like a scaffies lorry with their rubbish lying about but apart from that it was incident free.

WHERE DID IT GO WRONG

We arrived back in Camp late afternoon just in time to have our tea, but before that we had to come to terms with the fact that the Administration Block had been destroyed by fire!

All that was left were the brick foundations. The Guard Room, Admin Office and C.Os Office were gone. Quite a bit of disruption had been caused, but nobody cracked a light (pardon the pun) as to what happened. Many records must have been destroyed. Across the drive there was another row of huts they had been commandeered to house the people made homeless by the fire ie. The Sports Store which was the only other building with barred windows. This was turned into a Guard Room, the Guard Room was essential as it always had customers.

Leave over we settled into our old routine. I allowed myself to be led astray by my friend Phil. We were taking part in a twenty five mile route march. The whole battalion was involved. Phil decided he was going to throw a sickie the morning of the march. He persuaded me to do the same. The two of us arrived at the MI room at nine am. What a shock!

There were about twenty blokes ahead of us all with the same idea - skive the Route March. We were told to get in a line. Each was called into the Consulting Room. our names were taken and we were told to return to our Billet until further notice. I was wild with myself for being so bloody stupid. No doubt there would be repercussions. We were told to have lunch and then line up on the square wearing Full Service Marching Order (F.S.M.O.). We were to be forced to do a fifteen mile Route March with five minutes break every five miles. Normally it was a ten minute break every hour so we were being punished.

The two Sergeants in charge were on push bikes so the pace would be brisk, a kind of trot. I cursed myself all the way back to camp for being so bloody stupid and following on with the others, like a flock of sheep. My feet were sore. We were very tired and all because we thought we were smarter than our instructors.

I expected more repercussions when we had completed the march and was quite pleased that no further action was taken, a sore lesson was learned, but at the end of the day most of us were still daft kids I was still only fifteen and a half, we still had a lot to learn.

It was now half way through August and the harvest was in full swing. Behind the barracks there was a small farm. They were leading the crops home to the stockyard. Most of the work was being done by hand. The Combine Harvester was still in its infancy so the old fashioned methods were still in evidence. As I watched progress, I felt quite home sick We had always had a great time at the harvest and were allowed to muck in and help. How I longed to approach this farmer and ask if I could help. Sadly that area was out of bounds as was the West side of the camp where there were acres of Orchards. Once darkness fell we would sneak out and plunder a few apples.

The Old farmer and his wife were hard at it for at least two weeks from dawn till dusk. Their work produced eight to ten fairly large stacks (ricks). They then proceeded to thatch the tops to make them water proof, another two or three days work.

I used to check the Notice Board Daily to find out the latest happenings around the camp. One particular item caught my eye. It read if you have any experience of working on farms please contact your Platoon Sergeant. Mine at the time was appropriately named Sgt Farmer. I got a hold of him and asked for details. He explained that about two dozen blokes were required to help out with some farm work for two weeks. We would be paid the same rate as the

Army paid us. It meant two weeks at double pay. Yes put my name down! We had to be ready to start work at the Farm at eight thirty. We boarded the truck at seven thirty and arrived at eight fifteen, ready to start work. We were to be harvesting Flax, yes Flax. I had seen it grown at home but had never handled it. Oh well it was something new and a change from marching around a drill square.

Flax is a plant which was widely used during the war to make dressings out of fibres in the bulb at the top of the stalk. It is also used widely as health food. It can also be crushed and made into Linseed Oil so it is quite a useful plant, sadly no longer grown in the rich European Countries as cheaper man made fibers are readily available. The reason it was pulled by hand was to get the maximum length of the fibers which are found in the stalk so there you have it

It was pretty tedious work but the lure of the extra seventeen shillings and sixpence (77.5p) kept us working. Day two and the men were sorted out from the boys when five of our number reneged. By the following Monday we were down to nine but we hardy ex farm hands stuck it out. It was back breaking work and sore on the hands. No fancy gloves in the good old days.

Back to the routine in the camp and a full twenty Park Drive in my pocket. Life was a breeze but it can so easily get spoiled . The nights were closing in and we were into autumn. Most of the harvesting was finished. The Apples in the surrounding orchards were ready for plundering so it was another ploy to ease the boredom of polishing Boots and Brasses. Everything was quiet, the communal wireless was playing some pop music when suddenly one of the lads called out "Come till you see this" I could hardly believe my eyes. All the Hay Stacks on the little Farm were alight and burning furiously. I could hardly believe what I was seeing. They were well alight by the time a Fire Engine arrived, what a disaster for the owner! His year's work totally destroyed in less then twenty minutes. It appeared that the Police were treating the fire as suspicious. There was a lot of questioning going on. The next day the CID were in the camp for most of the day. Something was going on although we were kept in the dark.

We had another wonderful break that summer when we spent two weeks under canvas at a war time Aerodrome on the Lincolnshire coast. It was near to the River Humber called North Coats. The water was nearly a mile from the shore. That was a brilliant break.

Summer camp cookhouse under the guidance of Sgt Harris

The Aerodrome was now home to the RAF Regiment, although we saw very little of them. One of our guys had a lucky escape when he nearly drowned in the river. He was on his last legs when pulled from the water. I met this lad at a reunion fifty seven years later.

The day we left the camp site to return to our Barracks we had our mid-day meal at the RAF dining room. It was like the Ritz compared to what we were used to! Three choices of main meal. We were used to take it or leave it. How the other half live!

Back to the daily grind and the year was wearing on. Soon it would be October, our next leave would be Christmas. There was still no word as to how the haystacks went on fire, but the inquiry was still on-going. The CID was adamant that it was arson but catching the culprit was proving difficult. They recorded hundreds of statements but to no avail.

We had another treat in store when we were invited to attend a Military Tattoo in the city of Nottingham. That would be another adventure for us. Although our platoon was not performing we were to be used as ushers, showing people to their seats etc.

Once everybody was seated and the show began we were free to do as we pleased. Four of us opted to go back to our Marquee and get a cup of tea. As we strolled along between the tents and dressing Marquees, one of the guys lifted the corner of a tent and we were gobsmacked! Twenty five to thirty lovely young ladies, all in various stages of undress, an adolescent youth's dream come true. We settled down on the grass to admire our new found bit of luck.

Suddenly from lying flat on my stomach I was standing upright with a hand gripping my collar till it near strangled me. A voice hissing in my ear your are a filthy little pervert. I managed to swivel round and there was a six foot Military Policeman calling me the most awful names. We

41

were marched back to out Marquee and ordered to stay there for the rest of the evening, our names were taken but thankfully no further action was taken.

BORSTAL OR ARMY

Round about this time, autumn1953, there was a statement in the press stating that the youth of that era who were stepping out of line would be given a choice as an alternative to Borstal. They would be given the opportunity to join the Army Boys Service.

Ssadly the Army was lumbered with some really unsavoury characters. They didn't want to be in the Army but it got them off the hook. My next chapter will explain what I mean. The guys in the platoon I had been with since arriving at Tuxford were great. We never had any arguments and there was no thieving. Everybody got on well and looked after each other. Sadly that comradeship started to wane with the type of guys now arriving at the camp. Word soon got round the Barracks that we had an Irish guy who was a pure psychopath. His party piece was to pick an argument and, when his opponent was least expecting it, he would head butt the guy right in the face. Most of the guys were terrified of him and his side kick, a little Scots fellow from Glasgow. He took great delight in showing the other lads the scars on his hands and arms where he had been slashed with an open razor. Two very unsavoury characters.

There were about eighty to a hundred lads in the Lunch queue awaiting the doors to open. It was like a forest full of monkeys, all chattering at the same time. Suddenly all went quiet. The main door burst open and a well built young fellow entered. He had a bit of a swagger about him. It was the mad Irishman. Somebody mentioned that he had been released from jail that morning. Anyhow he just sauntered past the lads in the queue till he reached the front. Nobody said a word except for one or two guys who had the guts to hiss at him. The duty Sergeant had clocked what was going on. He crossed over to where our friend was standing. They exchanged words and the Sergeant pointed to the back of the queue. Suddenly the Irishman drew his head back and whacked the Sergeant in the face. He went down like a sack of potatoes - blood everywhere. One of the cookhouse staff called the Regimental Police and the thug was taken away.

If I remember it right, he needed four R.Ps to handle him, He was so dangerous that he spent a lot of his time tethered to a radiator in the Guard Room. He was given the maximum sentence allowed by the Company commander - twenty eight days.

This was this guy's third term in jail in about six weeks of service. Can anybody truly say he joined the Army to make a career for himself? I don't think so. His little Glaswegian mate was no better. They were full time jail birds.

It was getting near lights out when Phillip, my neighbor, announced he was going to the cook house for something to eat. We pointed out it was closed for the night. His reply was "Its got gless windeas,"

With that, he took off. Ten minutes later he was back with his arms full of food. He dumped it under the floor boards and off he went again. One of the guys leaving the washroom spotted Phil being escorted to the Guard Room. He had been caught. Stupid boy! he would get time for this.

Half -an- hour later Phil and an escort arrived in our billet where he picked up his gear and left. He was pretty sheepish. He had probably just realized what a bloody fool he had been. I tried to puzzle Phil's logic. We were never hungry - always plenty food. You could grab something in the Canteen until nine-o-clock. Eventually I came to the conclusion it was an act of bravado.

Although I had been in the next bed to Phil for nearly a year I knew very little about him. He never spoke about his family although I did find out he lived in Maryhill Glasgow and was one of a family of ten. Other wise he was anonymous. He was sentenced to seven days in the nick so he was in with the thugs who were each doing about twenty eight days.

We had another day of excitement, we wakened this particular morning, while getting dressed we were told to have our breakfast and return to our billet and await further instructions. Right away the comment was, "What the hell can be wrong now?" During breakfast we found out what was wrong. The NAAFI had been done over and a large amount of cigarettes and money stolen, the place was swarming with Civilian Police.

HEALTH &SAFETY WHAT'S THAT ?

We had been back in the Billet about an hour when we were told to report outside. We were brought to attention and marched to the gymnasium. We were told to form a single file and report to one of the line of desks along the far wall where there were about half-a-dozen desks. At each desk there stood a Policeman or a Detective. We were about to be finger printed. The whole camp was involved. After a day of Police activity we were allowed back into the NAAFI that evening, the Police had been unsuccessful. There were no arrests.

Phil arrived back in the billet after doing his time. I hoped he had learned his lesson. As usual he was full of the joys of spring. He started to empty his kit bag stowing away his goods and chattels in his locker as he neared the bottom of his kit back he leaned into it and pulled out a ten pack of woodbine.Half hiding the pack with his hand he passed it to me, muttering a present for you.

keeping it very secretive, at the time I didn't think much about it and enjoyed the smoke, a change from dog ends and roll ups, which amounted to about twenty percent tobacco and eighty per cent paper.

We had quite an exciting time ahead of us. Next week we were going to the Rifle Range for the first time. It didn't really do anything for me as I had no real interest in shooting but it was part of the training, so grin and bare it. Some of the lads couldn't wait to get there but not me.

Anyhow the day arrived and we picked up pack lunches from the Dining hall. Then we paraded outside the billet waiting on the transport which was three ton trucks. ,I can't really remember where it was but the name Ollerton rings a bell. The range was one thousand yards long with butts every hundred yards, about eight guys were shooting at the same time. The noise was horrendous. It came to my turn but I'm afraid the enemy need have no fear. My shooting was abysmal, although I could hit the target I was never near the Bulls Eye. My shoulder was in agony for days after and my hearing was badly affected. We had no ear defenders. They were not even invented then. Over the years I have ended up with a severe hearing problem, wearing hearing aids for over twenty years. My Audiologist discussed my working life to try and pinpoint what would have caused my hearing deterioration. She was quite adamant that my stint on the rifle ranges could have been the start of my problem. My brother-in-law who was a top ear, nose and throat surgeon was of the same opinion.

Although we were being trained to kill people with rifles, sten-guns, machine gusn, hand grenades and two sizes of mortar bombs not forgetting the the trusty old bayonet if all else failed. We were actually still daft young boys full of pranks I was still three months away from my sixteenth birthday in modern times we would still be in school.

This particular day we were dismissed for Lunch. Our billet was at the far end of the corridor so you can imagine twenty five robust youths jockeying for position as they raced along the corridor, I was one of the first three at the billet door as we pushed it open. What a shocker confronted us!

Unbeknown to us a local contractor was renewing part of the floor. He had about six or eight boards removed and left a gaping hole in the floor - no sign warning us of the danger. With the momentum of the guys pushing behind, a few of us fell into the hole which was six feet deep.The geests under the flooring saved us from crashing to the bottom, although the landing on the geests was pretty painful on the ribs.

The medic was called and he administered pain killers after a brief examination I was unable to continue the afternoon session. I was in so much pain and it was affecting my breathing The medic was adamant I hadn't broken any ribs. I was able to return next morning, although my ribs ached for months after that. The Medic suggested I had maybe cracked a rib. We had had a narrow escape if we had gone all the way through the hole which was approx six feet deep they could have had a fatality on their hands. Imagine half-a-dozen eight stone lads landing on top of you from six feet. The mind boggles.

Everything was settled down and going well. We were into the month of November 1953. It was getting colder but, with the training we were doing, we had no time to feel the cold. It would soon be Christmas and home for a leave.

We finished our morning session and were told to stay in the billet after lunch until we were called. The usual comment when this happened was, "What the hell's wrong now!" but, for a change, this was something different. We were marched to the recreation hall and told to find a seat. Somebody whispered, "another bloody lecture no doubt.".

Once we were all seated an officer got up and announced, "Gentlemen to-day the greatest Football team on the Planet are playing England in a friendly at Wembley Stadium. It is none other than the Hungarians, the Mighty Magyars. We have hired this contraption which I believe is called a television - not one of the more conventional ones. This one is rather unique".

He was correct in as much it was more like a cinema projector that beamed the pictures on to s six foot screen. I had never seen a Television before so this was new to me. Anyhow the game kicked off and it was sheer magic. All the way through the Hungarians were magicians especially Puskas. He scored goals with the greatest of ease. The Final Score Hungary six England three. England must have had quite a good team, to score three against the world champions was no mean feat. I have never forgotten that game, probably the best exhibition of football I have ever witnessed.

The excitement of the greatest Football game I have ever witnessed was over. It was back to basics. We were in for another surprise. At our field training the next day we were told that we had endured many hours of theoretical training and, one day soon, we would be able to 'have some practical experience.' We were going to attack and try and capture an Airfield.

The next few days were spent preparing for our assault. It was real interesting stuff.. The great day arrived and it was all systems go. We were all togged up in our battle gear and ready for the off. We were driven to within a mile of the Airfield which happened to be near Newark Nottinghamshire. The first thing that frightened the shit out of us was the Jets swooping low over head. The noise was horrendous. There was a big incentive for us, our commanding officer had offered a reward if any of us could capture the RAF Commanding Officer.

I can't remember how much it was. Five pounds rings a bell but even a pound would have been a fortune to us. We got down beside a burn and followed that till we came to a Bridge where we took cover. The RAF Boys were shooting at us with blanks but every now and again there was a ping like you would get from a live round. Some of our older Boys suspected the RAF guys were shoving broken pencils up the barrel to frighten the day lights out of us. We never did find out what it was. The Noise was still horrendous and quite nerve racking. Suddenly the RAF guys charged us from behind and we were captured. They marched us back to their Guard Room and crammed about thirty of us into quite a small cell. Then they turned the heating on full blast until we were nearly melted. These guys obviously had never heard of the Geneva Convention and the treatment of P.O.Ws . We were well and truly beaten but it was a great exercise and very enjoyable. It gave us an insight as to what a War Zone sounded like without bombs dropping all over the place.

Our C.O. Had an ace up his sleeve and probably saved the Army from getting a proper red face. One of our Education Sergeants, who was known as Zeke, was recruited as a spy for the day. He was the most unlikely looking person to be trained as a spy (but never judge a sausage by its skin as the saying goes). Zeke entered the RAF camp on a bicycle, carrying a tool bag. How he passed the guards I never ever found out but he convinced them he was there to check an electrical fault in the Control Tower. Once in, he had these little cardboard cards with bomb printed on them. He planted them all over the place remaining unobserved while he was there. Our C.O phoned his counter part and warned him to evacuate the Control Tower as it was due to blow up in twenty minutes time. Over all a good result for the Boy Soldiers.

Before I move on I would like to say a few words about our education tutor Sargent Zeke. I have already stated he looked the most unlikely Spy imaginable, but he was an excellent Tutor. After all my years at school I still learned more from Zeke than I did from anyone at school.. He was a smashing person.

The year was wearing on and we would be on leave shortly. There was a round of promotions. Four of our guys were made up to L/cpl , I was not one of them as I was not nearly dedicated enough - too much nonsense in my head! Everything was a great joke, I had a lot to learn. One of the highlights of my week was the Scottish country dancing. It was an evening class run by WO Sim, an Aberdonian in the Education Corps. Philip and I used to add extra moves in our routine. It was unconventional but the rest of the lads got a good laugh. I'm sure Mr Sim was near tearing his hair out with some of our antics. Funnily he never said anything, just shook his head.

It had been a few weeks since we last had a Police presence in the Camp but, Lo and Behold, a few days before we were due to go home, the place was swarming . What could be wrong this time? At the back of the Sergeant Mess the local Army Cadet Force had their hut. They carried out their meetings and stored their equipment there as well. It had been burgled and lots of items stolen. The weapons taken were useless apart from being props for training purposes. The biggest item taken was a machine gun. Most of the items had been dumped and were soon recovered , but the machine gun was still missing. The day we went on leave anybody carrying a kit bag was searched at the gate. lo and behold we had one brainless wonder in the battalion. His kitbag was found to be carrying the offending machine gun. It had been stripped down so that all the pieces would fit in the bag. I cant remember the punishment he received but he probably missed his leave or maybe opted for the cane.

My sixteenth birthday passed without incident. I would be due a pay rise. The money went up to one pound seven and six.(27/6) (£1 37.5p). As I try to remember back to that leave Christmas 1953, my mind is a blank, so the journey home and back must have been hassle free. I would soon have a year's service under my belt, I was enjoying it, but couldn't see myself as a career soldier. I didn't put enough interest into it, still too much nonsense in my head.

A NEW YEAR NEW DAWN

Back in camp we were soon into the swing of things. The only significant change was the construction of an Assault Course. It was built behind the camp, bringing a fairly wide burn into play as part of the obstacles. This should be interesting, although none of the obstacles seemed too difficult.

The latest intake of guys included two from my home area. One I already knew. They were both destined for the Gordon Highlanders. Everything was going to plan as far as I was aware. Although we had no pop music as we know it today from the fifties era, we still had our favorite music. This was pre transistor radio days, but our popular tunes were played on the wireless which was piped throughout the camp. Each billet had a speaker. The only draw back was, if you wanted to listen, it would be what somebody else had chosen.

Our main program was from eleven pm to midnight on a Sunday evening. Unfortunately it was lights out at ten pm. but some brave soul would sneak over to the Radio shack and switch the wireless back on just before eleven and, with a bit of luck, we would hear the whole show. Some nights the duty Sergeant would switch it off and we were left in limbo.

We had our favorite singers, mostly very sedate ladies like Doris Day, Ruby Murray, Rosemary Clooney and Theresa Brewer. The men were Frankie Laine, David Whitfield, Tex Ritter to name but a few. I said the ladies were sedate as they wore sensible clothes, not like the ones of today who have to show as much bum and t**s as is legal.

We had been back from our leave for three weeks or so and everything was going fine. I'm not sure of the date of this next happening but remember clearly at what time it happened. Our usual routine was supper between eight and nine pm, a quick tidy up to the uniform and boots maybe layout the outfit for next morning. Everybody in bed for lights out at ten pm. You could soon hear the snorers at work. Some of them were horrendous. By eleven everybody would be sound asleep. Being a Boy soldier was hard work so sleep came easy.

We had all been sleeping for about three hours when, all of a sudden, our sleep was disrupted and the nosiest little man I have ever heard was shouting at us to get up and head for our muster area as there was a fire. He could have wakened the dead. Cpl Bathgate of the Argyle and Sutherland Highlanders was noisy at the best of times but on this occasion he was at his best. Out on the square shivering with the cold we could not believe the devastation we were witnessing. We didn't shiver for long. The heat from the fire was tremendous, even from across the width of the Drill Square, it was quite hard to bare.

The recreation Room and all the lovely furnishings, books and games especially the full sized snooker table totally destroyed. I had spent many happy hours in that room. Then there was the NAFFI ablaze from end to end. Nothing could be saved. The camp was a wooden structure. No doubt gallons of Creosote had been used to coat the buildings. The original Creosote was highly inflammable. Once the flames took hold there was no stopping them. Funnily enough I have no recollection of the Fire Engines. We had a fire service in the camp but it would have been hard pushed to control a Chip pan fire. After about twenty minutes we thought we were being attacked. We think it was the tins of Brasso. They were like rockets flying up into the night sky. Once they were above the flames and probably hit the cold air they exploded - quite frightening as we couldn't see them. We were stood about for a couple of hours while they got things under control. The big fear was if it spread to any other buildings. There is no saying what tragedy would unfold.

Bear in mind the main living quarters (known as spiders) were all joined together. If they caught alight there would be no stopping them. As we returned to our beds, our thoughts were of what might happen should the fire flare up again.Tthe evenings happenings were a great tragedy. We had no respite for losing half a nights sleep. The noisy beggars were at it dead on six am, so we just had to drag ourselves out of bed and get on with it.

The cold light of day highlighted just how devastating fire is. The two buildings were ravaged to the ground. Anybody with the least bit of compassion would have felt a bit of sorrow seeing the beautiful recreation room reduced to ashes and the NAFFI reduced to heaps of rubble - sad,sad times. For days after the event we would find half burnt pound and ten shilling notes scattered around the camp.They had to be handed in, probably for insurance purposes.

There was a strong Police presence around the site of the fires. Then a strange thing happened. The Police requested to carry out another fingerprinting exercise. If you had been done first time round you were not required. There had been a couple of intakes since the NAFFI burglary so they were updating their records. The police had pinpointed the root of the fire. It had started in an arm chair in the recreation room so they were making progress. They had a real stroke of luck, they had a finger print from the burglary and they had a match. This arose from this second finger printing exercise and, believe it or not, it was from a guy who had been missed first time round. Why was he missed? Because he was in jail at the time and obviously the Police thought because he was in jail there was no way he could be involved. It's a rather interesting story. If you remember back to when the Administration Block was burnt to the ground, the only building in the Barracks with barred windows was the sports store. It was converted to hold prisoners in the absence of a proper guard room. What the Provo Staff had overlooked was the fact that the bars on the windows were on the inside, held on with probably four or six screws. Remove the screws and you were free. The three guys doing time were the Psychopathic Irishman, his Scottish side kick and my neighbor Phillip. Phillip was arrested later that morning and the other two were probably doing time anyhow - that seemed to be their specialty. All three were charged with burglary, stealing hundreds of Cigarettes and money. They were to be Court Marshaled. During the robbery they had removed the cell bars, climbed out, carried out their dastardly deed and climbed back in. They replaced the bars. The near perfect crime!

Hhow were they caught then? During their visit to the NAFFI they had worn socks on their hand, but, as is often the case, young guys will have the odd hole in their socks. This is what was supposed to have happened to this three guys. They eventually were sentenced to two years in Colchester Corrective Establishment-,the Army Nick.

The Police must have thought they had hit the jackpot when a few days later they made an arrest. The Arsonist had finally been caught. It was a relief for everybody. The latest fire was too close for comfort.

Very little would have triggered a tragedy. How there were no more buildings burned the night of the NAAFI fire nobody will ever know. Many of the other buildings were less than ten feet away. Anyhow hopefully the days of the fire raiser were over and he was safely locked up .

He was a big Scouser, a strange sort of fellow, very quiet. When questioned they asked him what his motive was. His answer was "I just enjoy watching things burn." It gave him a great kick". His case was tried in a Civil Court. He was sentenced to be detained under Her Majesty's Pleasure. This means his sentence would be decided by some sort of parole board. There is no set release date. I believe it is decided on the severity of the crime and his behaviour during his sentence. I'm not sure if this sentence is still used as it s years since I have heard of it

DISASTER STRIKES

I remember this morning like it were yesterday. At last it was our turn to have a go on the new assault course. There were approximately eight obstacles to be negotiated. This was fairly straight forward but it was an uneven playing field as far as I was concerned. By that I mean everybody was treated the same. You had same amount of packs and pouches regardless if you were five foot three or six foot. The obstacles were all the same height so we little guys had a bit of a struggle. There was no quarter given and we had to do the best we could .

The final obstacle on the run was a rope stretched between two trees across the burn. We had to make our way across, then it would be lunch break. The rope was about ten feet above the water and maybe fifteen to twenty feet wide. Sadly there was no instruction given as to the best way to cross. Did you dangle like a monkey or use your legs as well as your arms? I could feel the adrenaline pumping and was feeling quite apprehensive. There was one guy in front of me, a six foot Irish lad. He opted to cross hand over hand and negotiated it safely. He was at the other side when I was told to go.

I never did like heights, so climbing the ladder was my first touch of fear. Then I started to cross. Right from the word go my arms were aching, half way and I was in utter agony. Suddenly the big brainless Irishman started to pump the rope up and down thinking it was a great joke. I lost my grip and went crashing onto the floor of the burn which was strewn with boulders. I knew as soon as I landed I had done some damage to my left ankle.

The rest of the squad had a great bit of amusement at my misfortune until somebody realized I was hurt and a couple of guys came forward to help me get up the bank. The meat wagon (army ambulance) was sent for and I was carted off to the M.I. Room where the Corporal Medic assumed I had either broken or fractured my ankle, which was now badly swollen. Next move was a trip to Worksop Hospital. After being x-rayed it was confirmed I had a fracture. I was then put in plaster. Encased in the plaster was a caliper. I was given crutches and sent back to camp. I was in plaster for six to eight weeks. The only classes I attended were education and any field work that was conducted indoors. Otherwise I was left to my own devices, mainly sitting around the billet. It was quite disappointing as nobody really checked up on me. The boredom of sitting around all day could get quite depressing.

I got a call from the M.I. Room to be ready to travel to Worksop the next day to have my plaster removed . This I did. After removing to original plaster which was in bits they wrapped my ankle from toe to knee with a thinner plaster. I could now get my boot on and was walking quite normally. At the reception I was given an appointment card which indicated I had to return in fourteen days to have the final plaster removed. I near threw a wobbly when I noticed that the appointment was bang in the middle of my next leave. I told one of my mates, who asked to see the card. It was something like the eighth of the month so he got a Biro and added a one. It now became eighteenth. On the day of my appointment I was called up to the desk. Not a word was spoken, only to tell me to take a seat. I am sure the girl at the desk thought they had made a mistake and didn't highlight it. The plaster was removed and my leg was right as rain. I was back playing football and my favourite cross country running. I have never had any restrictions or even pain since the day the accident happened.

It was great to be back in full swing. I could see the training was advancing with new drill movements etc. Yes life was enjoyable once more.

We had yet another scandal when the Stores Corporal was arrested and placed in close arrest. Seemingly he had a great little scam going with the guy who picked up the slops from the kitchen. He usually arrived on site after breakfast with four empty Churns in his little trailer, he dumped them and picked up four full ones.

One morning the R.Ps did a check and one of the churns contained rations, bread, butter etc The Corporal was arrested and no doubt Court Marshaled, but because he was permanent staff it was kept low profile and he was more than likely sent back to his Regiment, The Lincoln-shires. He was a silly sort of fellow as he was pretty elderly and no doubt he would have been discharged and lost his pension etc. but it takes all kinds.

My euphoria was quickly dashed when I received a message telling me I had been put back a squad with effect from Monday morning. I was gutted. I had been with the same platoon for fourteen months. We were like brothers with no animosity, fighting or squabbling. Everybody got on well and, one of the main things, there was no thieving. We had lost two guys, the little fellow who wet the bed and Phillip. Otherwise we were intact. Now this! I was heartbroken

Although Fifteen Platoon was next door I didn't know any of them. The way I got the message I felt was rather heartless. Surely this was an important move for me and a bit of the personal touch would have softened the blow. After all I had only just passed my sixteenth birthday but it was maybe a hard lesson to learn.

My welcome to Fifteen Platoon did nothing to help my depressive state. On dumping my kit on the vacant bed a voice from behind me stated, " We don't want any effing rejects in this Platoon!" A little mouth piece if ever there was one. I just ignored him and got on with my unpacking. The

59

bed space I was allocated was surrounded by Scots lads - three of them from near my home area. In fact I had been in the Boy Scouts with one guy so that wasn't too bad. Saturday evening and suddenly a rumpus broke out. Two of the biggest guys in the platoon decided to fight. They were each armed with a razor blade, I had never seen anything like this before. Where I came from a fight was two blokes facing up to each other, using their fists.

These two brandishing blades were circling one another but no action took place - a bit of bravado if you ask me. It all quietened down and we got back to polishing the kit. The next day was Sunday, time for Church Parade. I had only attended Church Parade for three weeks. When I first arrived at Tuxford one of the old Scottish sweats told us that we could go to Retford by truck and choose what you wanted to do - whether you be Catholic, Jewish or the Salvation Army. He said, "If anybody asks you tell them Salvation Army but we don't go to a church we head for a Cafe and chat up the birds." Next day we would try this ploy. We were all on parade. The R.S.M called out Church of England Parade Attention, he then said all other denominations fall out. This we did and headed for the three tonner parked at the side of the square. We hopped aboard and had a wonderful couple of hours away from the camp. Nobody ever queried us which was just as well because I never found out where the Salvation Army Hall was situated.

I remember one story from the Church Parade. On the Sunday morning as far as I remember the RSM was in charge. There were also four senior staff probably a Captain, Lieutenant and two second Lieutenant's or along those lines. On entering the Church there were two offering plates, one for each side of the aisle. The four top guys would each place half-a-crown (12.5p) in the plate and pass it on to the Boys. An NCO would follow the plate to the back of the church and, when complete, the NCO would walk down the aisle and place the plates in front of the Minister who would bless them.

On this one occasion there were only three half-crowns. One of the guys had nicked the fourth one - pretty low life that would steal off the Lords table. The culprit was never caught.

Although I was unhappy at being moved, I had to knuckle down and get on with it. There were some good lads in the squad. Six of us were Scots. Four of the six were from the North East of Scotland, so we four spoke the same lingo. Three of the guys were sexual deviants in other words one was Homosexual the other two would probably be classed as paedophiles because of their craving for pornographic reading material - nothing too serious in those days - Hank Jensen being one of the more popular authors. The rest of the squad were normal guys but there was not the same camaraderie I had enjoyed in fourteen platoon.

The lad in the next bed space to me was from the Buchan area. He was from a similar background to me. Charlie was still as broad as could be and the English guys had difficulty understanding him. He suffered a horrendous bit of bad news when handed word that his mother had died suddenly. He was on his way home within a couple of hours but had to face a twelve to fourteen hour journey, wondering what lay ahead of him. He was heartbroken. He was away for about a week. When he got back he discovered his locker had been robbed and the Camera his mum had given him the day he left home was gone. I don't think it was ever traced.

Shortly after my transfer we had a barrack room inspection. This was carried out by our Platoon Commander who was Lt Hawkins. We waited with baited breath, worried he would pick up some misdemeanor and if he did you were liable to be on a charge. Three or so beds from me he started to poke in this lads locker with his stick. A couple of minutes later he emerged with a ball of shredded newspaper on the end of the stick. Inside the ball were about four or five little pink mice. Our officer just about blew a fuse. He ordered the offender to be taken to the wash room and scrubbed clean. Some of the guys took great delight in this exercise. I felt sorry for the lad as it could have been any of our lockers.

As I said previously there were six Scots in the new platoon. We tended to stick together. The camaraderie was different from my original platoon.The six of us couldn't have been more different but four of us were destined for the Gordon Highlanders. Big Jock, an Aberdeenshire lad, was posted to Cyprus where he saw active service during the troubles there. Some of the earlier Boy Soldiers were also to see service in Cyprus. As I said one of the lads was homosexual, very effeminate, a strange lad but he had been brought up in orphanages all his life so the chances that he had been abused were quite high.

I quite liked the guy. Just because he was different didn't mean you shunned him, so I would keep him company at time. He never showed any tendencies to use his strange behavior towards me. One thing I found fascinating was that he always had money and cigarettes, when the rest of us would be broke. At times, mostly evenings, he would disappear. He would never say where he went or where he had been. One day he offered me a cigarette. it wasn't a cheap one either. I asked how he managed to be so well off . He was reluctant to tell me but eventually opened up and told me he did chores for one of the Sergeants. On asking what the chores were, he hedged his answer, but said "what ever the Sergeant needed doing.

His next question was " Would I be interested in helping out?". I jumped at the chance , he said he would talk to the Sergeant and let me know if he needed me.   Cecil (not his real name) approached me a couple of days later and said the Sergeant would like to see us that night. We agreed to meet at six pm and he would show me where to go. The Sergeant had a little room at the end of one of the billets. Cecil knocked and we stood for two or three minutes before this gruff voice shouted for us to enter. On his door was his name and his regiment, the Cameron Highlanders. He was sitting at a table or desk which was covered by a green Army issue blanket. His lower half was hidden under the blanket. He motioned for us to sit down and proceeded to study a piece of paper.

I was getting a bit agitated as the silence was deafening. He eventually spoke, asked my name and where I came from, then the usual chit chat. At that point the blanket moved slightly. This caught my eye immediately. Then the seam of the blanket parted ever so slightly and I could see an eye looking at me, the blanket was quickly sealed again. I was shocked. What kind of games were these guys up to? I didn't wait to find out but got up and left, The Sergeant's parting words were "Is there a problem?" .I didn't answer. I was sweating with fear when I landed back in the corridor. nothing like this had ever happened to me before. In fact I was so naive I had no idea that this sort of thing took place. The incident was never discussed. Cecil never mentioned it but I was certain I knew the owner of the eye under the blanket.

The big scandal of the day was the Lord Montague case where a party of men were deemed to have taken part in Homosexual Activities. Lord Montague, a leading peer in the UK, was jailed along with some of his fellow participants At that time it was a highly illegal act. A few weeks later our friend the Sargent was arrested and appeared in a civil court in Nottingham. He was sentenced to two years imprisonment. About a month later, yet another staff member was arrested and the same fate befell him. He was a Corporal in the

Queens Regiment and also received a two year sentence. I forget what the charges were but it was to do with sexual activities with under age boys..

Back to the day job of training us to be soldiers. Our next big adventure was an overnight exercise in Sherwood Forest sleeping in trenches and feeding ourselves for twenty four hours. This sounded great stuff except we hadn't taken into consideration the cold and possibly wet conditions we would encounter. We had just started to settle down when the rain started. This later turned to sleet and it was cold. Nothing much happened until the middle of the night about four am to be exact. We were roused and told to get ready for a patrol. We set off. It was good to be moving and get the circulation going.

We were creeping along in the near pitch dark when a young deer took off, startling the daylights out of half the squad. Big Scotty got such a fright he pulled the trigger and loosed off a round. Thankfully it was blanks, otherwise we would have had a casualty on our hand. This was an experience that I would not look forward to repeating in a hurry.

Life was never really the same for me in Fifteen Platoon, we all seemed to be in little cliques, each sticking to his own. The Scots and the Geordies were the most predominant. The Geordies had their fair share of bully boys. Another down side was the fact you could not leave anything of value lying around as it was sure to walk - not a very nice environment to live in - but we just had to grin and bear it.

The next incident, I am about to write about, was really the straw that broke the Camel's back for me.

My mother would send me a parcel every four to six weeks. It would contain a home baked cake and my beloved Sunday Post Newspaper. This kept me abreast with the Scottish Football and of course any outstanding News. On this occasion I arrived in the billet full of the joys of spring, made even more joyful when I noticed I had another parcel. Good old mam! It looked a bit tattered but that was not unusual. I tore the string off and near burst into tears when I saw the content. The cake had been battered into crumbs and my beloved Post torn into postage stamp size pieces. I was totally devastated. How could they do this? I was quite homesick at times and the parcels would cheer me up no end. This was downright wickedness. I had a notion as to who had done it but could say nothing. If you reported any incidents you were looked upon as a grass. This incident left me depressed for days. What kind of sicko would want to destroy other people's property? Especially something so sacred to me. Was it jealousy or downright wickedness? I just felt like packing it all in and going home.

I had a really bad bout of homesickness and very little would have persuaded me to go. During my fourteen months in fourteen platoon, we lost two guys the bed wetter and Phillip otherwise we had a full complement of the same guys from day one The spaces were filled, so we had a full squad of twenty five. But the class of recruits must have been slipping as at that point there was a billet with over twenty guys waiting discharge. Many of them could have been boys who were given the opportunity to enlist instead of going to borstal. Once the threat was off them they would then start working their ticket. But what was the point of signing up in the first place? If you found out you didn't like being a soldier you could buy yourself out at a cost of one hundred and twenty five pounds - a lot of money in the fifties. If you went the other way and tried to work your ticket you could end up with a black mark against your name and this could go against you, when trying for a job, so you had to be careful.

DEVASTATED

The date was first of May 1954. I had been in the Army for sixteen month come the six of May. Everything was sailing along quite smoothly. I still didn't like being in fifteen platoon but, if you kept to your own little clique, it was bearable. This was pre computer, pre tablet and pre mobile phone. Most of the orders and correspondence was carried out via the Notice Boards around the camp. One of the guys in the billet asked me if I had checked the notice board that afternoon. It was a Friday and the following week's activities were posted. I rushed round to where the board was situated and, after careful scanning, noted my name printed under the following Tuesday. I had to attend a medical in Nottingham at eleven am. The name of the place was stated and I would be picked up by transport at nine forty five from our MI room.

Right away I surmised it would be a check up on my fractured ankle as I had had no other medical problems or been to the MI room since my ankle injury. The Medic in the MI room could throw no light on the matter just for me to be ready at the stated time. I have no recollection of the journey to the City of Nottingham, only being in this huge building with lots of people milling about and endless office doors. I was shown to an office. On the door was a name plate with rank name and medical qualifications.

The only part I remember is that it said Lt Col Royal Army Medical Corps. I saluted and the Colonel told me to be seated. It was quite nerve wracking as he didn't say much, just looked at me. I was still of the impression I was there to talk about my fractured ankle but, strangely, it was not mentioned. I was in the office about twenty minutes. I had answered all his questions and was ready to go when he hit me with a bombshell calling me by my christian name he said, " Would you like to leave the Army Albert?" I was taken aback. Nobody had mentioned that I would be asked if I wanted to leave the Army but, in the heat of the moment, I said "Yes Sir." He wrote something in a folder and told me that would be all. I had no idea what the outcome would be.

On the Friday of that week one of the guys came rushing in and asked me " Have you seen the latest orders on the notice board ?" I shook my head and he advised me to have a look. I could hardly believe my eyes. I would be discharged the following Tuesday. I should make sure all my kit was cleared before I left. I was called into an office and advised that I would get no money until the Thursday. They didn't hold any money in the Camp after all the burglaries that had taken place. I was quite welcome to stay until Thursday but I was free to leave on Tuesday.

I had a quick think and said, " I'll go on Tuesday" Another lad, from Hull, was going the same day so we would travel to York together. We left the barracks after breakfast and headed for the village where we would get a bus to Retford. I was still reeling from the shock of what was happening to me. At no point did I fall foul of the authorities, I never went sick or caused any trouble so what was the reason for my discharge?.

Sadly I cannot recall the name of my companion. He had been in the Army a lot less time than me but he hated it and was delighted to be getting out. We pooled the few pence we had between us. After a couple of cups of tea we were left with probably about three shillings (15p). When we arrived at York my friend gave me his share of the pennies. He would be home in next to no time,

I still had twelve hours travel in front of me. By the time I got to Edinburgh I was starving so decided to break out and bought a pie and a cup of tea, I had a couple of fags which I smoked sparingly trying to make them last. When we left Edinburgh I was almost skint with just three or four pennies left. The hunger had left me but the future looked bleak food wise. Two fellow passengers joined the train at Edinburgh. They were headed for Arbroath,- RAF guys on leave from Cyprus. They were full of chatter and let me know they had cheated Customs and managed to get a few hundred fags home duty free. I didn't say much to them as they were in the lap of luxury and I was skint,with something like four pence in my pocket and still had hours of travel. I hoped to be home by lunch time.

BACK TO WHERE I STARTED

We were getting close to Arbroath when I decided to try my luck at begging I asked the two guys if they could lend me a pound. I explained my predicament and left it at that. They squirmed about uncomfortably but didn't commit themselves. I had promised to return it as soon as I got home if they would just give me their home address. There was ,still no comment. The silence was embarrassing so I decided to go to the toilet. This would allow them to discuss my request. The train was slowing down for the Arbroath stop when I returned to the carriage. They stood up ready to go when one handed me sixpence (2.5p). The other had two Prize Crop cigarettes in his hand. He handed them to me as they left the carriage.

Feeling a bit sarcastic it was on the point of my tongue to ask for an address, so that I could send the tanner back to the miserable pair of blank blanks! But we should be grateful for small mercies.

We arrived in Aberdeen at an ungodly hour of the morning.My bus for Banff was due at six am, so I had a bit of a wait. I knew there was an early morning Cafe at the Harbour where you could get a cup of tea and a buttered rowie (Aberdeen Buttery). So, at the back of four, I made my way along to the Café. I had managed to scrape ten pennies together. My purchase came to nine pennies (4.5p) the hot tea was a godsend and the wifie behind the counter was an angel as she gave me a second cup for free.

I boarded the bus at six am and arrived in Banff just after nine. I then had to go four miles into the country before I got home. ,I was too tired to walk so I went to the local garage and hired a taxi, hoping my mother could pay the fare as I was totally skint.

Mother made a big fuss getting the frying pan on and

69

a bacon and egg fry up. Unfortunately I was past being hungry and had great difficulty eating so I found a vacant bed and collapsed into it and slept soundly until late afternoon. The young brothers and sisters arrived home from school and were so pleased to see me, We had a great evening and it was soon bed time again.

Next morning I was in the real world - no job, no idea how to get a job as I had no experience at anything. The only skill the Army taught me was how to shoot people and there were no vacancies for that type work. Thursday arrived and a letter with OHMS I tore it open and found a cheque for twenty eight pounds. My final pay off from her Majesty's Forces. At least I was solvent for the time being. Friday morning was the day the situations vacant were published in the Local Press. I went to the shop and got a paper and, during a browse, I noticed an advert for youth aged sixteen for labouring work at a sawmill about four miles from home. On a borrowed bicycle I set off to find out if the post was still vacant (No Mobiles then). It was a fairly hilly route and then one mile through a forest track.It took about forty minutes. I could hear the noise of the Circular saw from a mile away. Situated in the middle of the forest it was dead silent so the noise of the saw seemed to be louder than normal. The guy working the saw was probably in his forties, five foot eight in height.

He stopped working and came over to speak to me. I enquired about the job and told him I had no experience. He told me the rate of pay was Two shillings per hour 2/- (10p) and it was a fifty hour week. He showed me what I was expected to do and asked if I was interested. My training had lasted about all of twenty seconds but the job was not Rocket Science. I asked when he wanted me to start, "Monday morning at seven am would be fine."

Leaving the house at six fifteen, I would be there in

plenty of time. I could hear the saw as soon as I entered the Forest..He was already working. My job was to clear away the cut timber and build it into stacks. The Sawmiller acknowledged my arrival with a curt wave of his hand and kept his noisy machine screeching as it chewed its way through the timber.In front of me was a mound of Pit Props, two by two square by three feet long . I had to load them on a flat barrow and wheel them to an area where I stacked them to a height of six feet. Lunch break finally arrived and I thought at least I would get a blether as I hadn't spoken a word since I said goodbye to my mother at six am. I dug out my lunch bag and sat down thinking my boss may join me.

But I would remain mute the rest of the shift. He got seated behind his saw and, while he had his lunch, he sharpened the blade. It was impossible to speak with the noise the file made as it rasped along the teeth. Our half hour over. It was time for another four and a half hours of torture.

This was my first day of carrying out manual labour. I thought five-o-clock would never arrive. I was aching from head to toe. Muscles appeared I didn't know existed. The four mile cycle home was sheer agony. After three days the aches and pains started to disappear as my body got used to the work but it was soul destroying and the fact the boss never stopped to have a blether was disappointing. There was no improvement in the conditions the following week. It was very depressing. If the work had even been interesting it would have helped, but what is interesting about a lump of timber? After the initial inspection what else is there to look at? Into my third week and on the Friday morning it was howling a gale, very difficult to cycle against. Once I entered the Forest I could see the Sawmill from about half a mile away. A scene of horror was to greet me that morning. The gales had blown over all the stacks of timber in the yard. It was all in a tangled heap. This was again the straw that broke the camel's back. I decided I would look for another job.

The local paper on Friday had a job I could possibly manage, working on a Pig farm with no experience necessary. I phoned the contact number and was told to come and see the man next day which was Saturday. It was awkward to get to, so I cycled over on the afternoon, a distance of 5/6 miles. The farmer was a rather obnoxious character and he took advantage of my inexperience when it came to money. It was a live- in position. I would get all my food and there was a Bothy to sleep in which was in good condition. I agreed to start on the Monday morning. My first chore was to feed the two hundred pigs, muck out the battery hens, then make my way to the Turnip field where I would spend the next six hours pulling up turnips and topping and tailing them.

It didn't take me long to realise that I had leapt from the Frying Pan into the Fire - another dead end, brain dead job.

The Boss turned out to be a big fat bully who was not averse to raising his hand if he was in a nasty mood, or if he was drunk. I experienced his wrath one Sunday Morning near Christmas when, in a hungover state, he lashed out at me because he thought I was dragging my heels.

After that outburst I decided enough was enough. I had jumped out of the frying pan into the fire. It was too near the end of the year to change jobs again but as soon as we were into the next year I would be on the move. This guy was taking advantage and, because I was destitute, I had no options but stay. At least I was having my food and the pittance he was paying me.

My oldest brother worked on the Construction Sites in the Highlands. He was coming home for the New Year. I made arrangements to go and visit him and discuss the chances of getting work on the Sites. We met up and he said he would have a word with his bosses and see if they would take me on. I had just celebrated my seventeenth birthday. Shortly after the New Year I got word to start work the following week. Before I left my sadistic friend I needed some form of revenge to even things up in line with the slap he had given me a few weeks before.. I lay on my bed planning in my evil mind. Yes I had it! I would work till the Saturday and then on Saturday evening I would pack my few belongings and leave without telling him. It was my weekend for looking after the cattle, unpaid may I add. On the Sunday morning he would find out I was no longer there and would have to do all the graft alone. I bet he was dancing with rage but hell mend the unpleasant excuse for a human being!

It was quite wintry when I arrived at the Construction Site where they were building a Hydro Dam. My brother had fixed me up with a bed in the twenty five bed billet. When we opened the door the smell of sweaty feet was over-powering. It took your breath away. Everybody wore welly boots and, instead of ordinary socks, they wore Donegal Socks which were basically pieces of blanket wrapped round the feet. They were warm and cheap. Everybody had two sets, one drying and one being worn.

So with twenty five pairs of Donegal Socks being dried, the smell was quite pronounced. I took to the Construction Site. No bother. The Billet had twenty five residents. There was company twenty four hours a day, a bit like the Army.

My joy was short lived. Due to severe snow storms the camp was closed for a few weeks, but, for the next eighteen years, I worked all over the Highlands and even managed a couple of years in England. The down side was having to live away from home a lot of the times. By this time I was married to Jessie. We had met in the village Hall in Invergarry in February 1957 and were married the same year. Living apart was not very pleasant for the wives but, if you wanted a decent pay packet every week, it was a sacrifice that had to be made, I always tried to get home every week-end.

Even after twenty years in the Construction Industry we were still considered semi-skilled which meant lower rates of pay than guys who had learned a trade. This used to gall me as some of them were downright lazy but that is the uneven split of the world .

Then in 1972 the Americans struck oil in the North Sea. Within months there was a big recruitment drive. Men between the ages of eighteen and sixty were being interviewed and offered different posts. The Americans set up training schools and trained their own tradesmen, mostly Welders and Fitters but there was a variety of other employment on offer. \painters were in big demand. I got an application form and applied, sat the exam and had the medical. I was offered a post as a trainee welder. ,I was now thirty five years of age. It never occurred to me that the standard of welding would be so stringent.

Eight weeks after starting I passed my first welding test, tested to the highest American Welding Society testing procedure. My clock number was forty one so I got in early. I took to the welding like a duck takes to water and really enjoyed it, but my welding skills were severely curtailed when I was offered a position as a Leaderman less than six months after qualifying. My first step on the promotion ladder. For the next twenty seven and a half years I worked on some of the biggest projects built for the North Sea.

Before I retired, I had learned to operate a computer This was a god send to me as it was another hobby I could spend time on, I had always been a bit of an action man working, gardening and having a good time at the week-ends. So this heart attack business had left me twiddling my thumbs at

74

times. But with my computer I could turn my hand to writing poetry. I have written many poems, mostly topical stuff and I published a book of my works.

In 2003 I got introduced to the Normandy Veterans Association. They invited me to join them on a trip to France where we would visit the Cemetery where my father is buried. I spent seven wonderful years with the Veterans, traveling to Europe and attending parades both here and on the Continent. It was brilliant and most enjoyable, sadly not many are left. age has taken its toll.

IBB/ IJLB ASSOCATION

During one of my Computer sessions, I was just trawling through some Army stuff when a certain Document caught my eye, it read, were you a boy soldier? if so, we want to hear from you. The address was to a certain Charlie McGrogan the Chairman of the Association. I thought my involvement with the Infantry Boys Battalion was long past. It was now Forty Nine years since I had left the battalion but it was worth investigating. I replied to the email and explained that my total service was eighteen months, so I was unsure if I would qualify. Back came a reply and an application form. They were to have a re-union at Milton Keynes TA Barracks in October, costing Fifteen Pounds . I asked Charlie if many lads from Tuxford were attending, Charlie being a bit of a leg puller assured me there would be quite a few.

It turned out there were three of us. Because of my eyesight and hearing problems and of course the aging process I gave up driving on motorways years ago. To get to Milton Keynes I had to use trains and, from my home in Inverness, that was about a ten hour journey. I was quite apprehensive but arrived at the T.A. Barracks on the outskirts of town about five pm. There were two guys in front of me, a fellow Scot and Ex Gordon Highlander Bill Morrison. The other lad was Dennis Healy. I was delighted to see them. Up until that point I felt a bit lost but we soon got cracking. They had served their Boys Service at Plymouth. The rest of the lads started to arrive in dribs and drabs but there were none that I knew and none who had served at Tuxford.

The TA Barracks was a brilliant set up and, if you were interested, you could have a bed for the night as opposed to one of the local hotels. I chose the barracks as it was handier than finding a hotel at mid-night, probably half

76

pissed and in my case Knackered..

Sleeping arrangements Milton Keynes T. A.

Charlie McGrogan and his entourage arrived around seven pm. I could hardly believe that I recognized one of them right away. Bob Ritchie had been a Boy Cpl at Tuxford. We got talking and Bob told me he had completed forty years associated with the Black Watch and retired as Major. Some achievement! Sadly Bob passed away a couple of years ago I miss his craic on Facebook.

The other Tuxford lad was Lofty Knight whom I couldn't remember from our service days. I made one lasting friendship with the late Mike Prince, a lovely big lad who shared the same interests as me in touring Europe and visiting some of the WW2 Battle fields etc. The next morning we headed for a Motorway Cafe where we had a huge cooked breakfast before our dispersal and returning to our various home areas, I still keep up to speed on Facebook with some of the lads I met at Milton Keynes .

I attended the next two re-unions at Milton Keynes. That would have been 2006 and 2007. The 2007 gathering was well attended with quite a lot of guys from around Oswestry, This is the Barracks where the Boy Soldiers were stationed the longest. At the AGM it was strongly contested to move the annual get together to the Parkhall Barracks Oswestry. It was a unanimous decision that the next meeting in 2008 would be in Shropshire. We were sitting having a drink after the AGM and the meal, just meeting different lads and a couple of lasses when I found myself next to a gentleman who had a similar accent to myself. I asked him where he came from, he said " A little village in the North East of Scotland nae doot you have never heard of it" My reply was "try me". He said, "It's called Cullen." I had to ask him to repeat it. "Oh I've heard of it ok I was born there in 1937."

I had just made friends with Ken Nicol. He was ten years younger than me so our paths would never have crossed in our tiny village but it's a small world. The 2008 re-union was well attended. At the AGM a decision was taken to build a Memorial in memory of the lads who served and the ones who gave their lives in the various conflicts. It was a mammoth task but a date was set for a week-end in June 2009 for a re-union. The planners did a splendid job and organized a Parade through the town of Oswestry.

IBB/IJLB Memorial Dedicated on the 7th
June 2009. Situated in the Cae Glas Park in
Oswestry Shropshire

The Parade on Dedication Day
Marching Through Oswestry Town Center

THE GRAND PARADE

The big week-end incorporating the Dedication of the Memorial and the re-union were scheduled to take place in Oswestry on the week-end of the six and seventh of June 2009. The Committee had done a sterling job getting everything organized. The week-end went like clockwork. My wife and I left Inverness on the morning of the fifth of June arriving in Wrexham around six-o-clock in the evening. My friend Ken was supposed to meet us at the Station and drive us to Oswestry, but due to yet another late train we had to change plans at the last moment and go by taxi.

Our Hotel, the Sebastian, was in the old part of the town quite a charming setting. We were in a Chalet at the back so not much of a view but everything was brand new just ideal for us ,we like the peace and quiet.

Saturday the sixth of June was to be quite busy with an AGM at eleven-o- clock in the Wynnstay Hotel, then on to the old Parkhall Barracks where we were having our re-union, there was a Buffet available and it gave us time to meet up with the other people attending. There were only four Ex Tuxford guys as far as I remember, but everybody was very friendly and I met countless people who I had got to know through Facebook. There was also at least half-a-dozen north Guys from around Inverness. Some of whom I met for the first time. The get together broke up late afternoon. It was back to the Hotel with just enough time to get dressed up ready for the Dinner again back in the Parkhall Gymnasium, now used as a Rugby Social Club .

I forgot to mention it had been steadily raining since early morning getting quite heavy by afternoon. Fingers crossed it would cease before the Big Parade in the morning. The dinner was just like the rest of the week-end so far, well organized.

At our table was Ken and Barbara, the chap who played the Pipes. I think he was Pipe Major Joe Kerr Ex Gordon Highlanders. There was also the lady who designed the memorial and her partner as well as my wife and I. We were a pretty mixed company.

We had a lovely evening. There were a few speeches and a few drams. Then it was back to the hotel and bed. We had an early morning ahead of us. Just before I turned in I checked the weather and it was still raining fairly hard.

Wakened at the crack of dawn next morning, there was no need to check the weather. The rain could be heard battering against the roof of the Chalet but it was early. Do not despair.

Our parade started mid morning. As we got ready there was no let up in the rain. It was quite heavy as we lined up to march the short distance to the Park which housed our Memorial. There were about three hundred on parade. It was quite eerie as three hundred rubber clad feet hit the tarmac as opposed to the Tackity Soled boots used by the regular Army, the Parade Commander would have cringed at the disorganized rabble that came to attention on his Command but we all did our best. The march to the Park went without incident but still it rained what a pity as everything else went like clockwork. After the Dedication and a short Service we were marched back to the Square and dismissed that was it all over.

In the evening my wife and I were invited to have a meal in the company of Ken and Barbara, Michelle and Roger, Janice and Sandy. The ninth person was on his own. He resided in Norway but his name escapes me. Next morning we were on our way to Cornwall to continue our holiday.

The re-union in 2010 was in the same venue. We attended the week-end. It was brilliant again along with friends Kenand Barbra and Sandy and Janice. The down side to the week-end for us was the journey. It needed eight train journeys. Getting on and off is a nightmare for my wife.Add to that the fact that the trains were all late, causing us to have to rush between platforms. It puts a damper on the week-end.

Sadly I have been unable to visit Oswestry again and, probably due to age catching up on us, it is doubtful if we will make the journey again but I will still keep up to date with Facebook just to see how everybody is getting on.

But it was brilliant while it lasted. I have a special word to say about Sandy and Janice. I had to attend Hospital in Edinburgh. This lovely couple offered me a bed for the night before my appointment. I was very grateful for this kind gesture.

I am getting near the end of this account of my life as a Boy Soldier, it was without doubt an experience. My one outstanding achievement that springs to mind is that I was the first boy Soldier allowed to wear civilian clothes . This came about when the Army sanctioned the wearing of a Blazer, Flannel Trousers, Plain Shirt and Tie black leather shoes. Once you purchased the outfit you had to do a mannequin parade in front of the Company Commander who would approve or disapprove. My tie was rejected as being too loud so I had to buy a plain one which I had approved. Soon I was overwhelmed by guys asking to borrow my outfit, so I put a charge on the hire. Half-a-Crown (12.5p) for an evening.It turned out to be a nice little earner.

AFTERWORD

At the age of Fifteen in nineteen fifty three, looking back I feel that the people from my part of the country were not as street wise as the City dweller's but on joining the Boys Service you soon learned sometimes it was the hard way. My length of service lasted for exactly eighteen months. I enjoyed every minute of it although at times it was difficult . In my opinion it was the best move I ever made as it gave me a great grounding for the rest of my life. In two months time (if I'm spared) I will be eighty years old. It is now sixty three years since I was discharged from the Army. The reason given -. Ceasing to fullfil Army Medical requirements.

     I am still vexed as to what that means as I went on to work for forty six years. My work took me to some of the most hostile areas in the Scottish Highlands where we faced very harsh conditions. Tthe West Coast is notorious for gales and lots of rain, but I never had a day's illness that caused me to be unable to attend work.

     I am always punctual to the point that I'm always waiting for other people. It is irritating. I keep myself and my clothes in immaculate condition and I try to be helpful and polite to anybody in need. These are all things that were taught to us as Boy Soldiers. It would do many of the young people of to-day the world of good and maybe make the world a better place for our young ones to grow up in.

     My longest stretch of employment was twenty seven years in the Oil Industry, where I held many posts in different disciplines. From the age of twenty two my employment was usually in Supervision, as a Manager or similar posts. I would put my skill in management down to what I learned in the boys service. This book is about my time as a Boy Soldier. Every incident is true . The only area that is maybe debatable is the dates. It is so long ago that some of the exact dates elude me. I hope who ever reads this book enjoys the contents. It is from a different world from what we have to-day. Thank you.

The Infantry Boys Battallion and Junior Leaders Batallion Association Plaque